Cambridge Elements

Elements in Economics of European Integration
edited by
Nauro F. Campos
University College London and ETH-Zürich

FROM CLUB TO COMMONS

Enlargement, Reform and Sustainability in European Integration

Veronica Anghel
European University Institute

Erik Jones
European University Institute and Carnegie Europe

Shaftesbury Road, Cambridge CB2 8EA, United Kingdom

One Liberty Plaza, 20th Floor, New York, NY 10006, USA

477 Williamstown Road, Port Melbourne, VIC 3207, Australia

314–321, 3rd Floor, Plot 3, Splendor Forum, Jasola District Centre, New Delhi – 110025, India

103 Penang Road, #05–06/07, Visioncrest Commercial, Singapore 238467

Cambridge University Press is part of Cambridge University Press & Assessment, a department of the University of Cambridge.

We share the University's mission to contribute to society through the pursuit of education, learning and research at the highest international levels of excellence.

www.cambridge.org
Information on this title: www.cambridge.org/9781009499200

DOI: 10.1017/9781009499194

© Veronica Anghel and Erik Jones 2025

This publication is in copyright. Subject to statutory exception and to the provisions of relevant collective licensing agreements, with the exception of the Creative Commons version the link for which is provided below, no reproduction of any part may take place without the written permission of Cambridge University Press & Assessment.

An online version of this work is published at doi.org/10.1017/9781009499194 under a Creative Commons Open Access license CC-BY-NC-ND 4.0 which permits re-use, distribution and reproduction in any medium for non-commercial purposes providing appropriate credit to the original work is given. You may not distribute derivative works without permission. To view a copy of this license, visit https://creativecommons.org/licenses/by-nc-nd/4.0

When citing this work, please include a reference to the DOI 10.1017/9781009499194

First published 2025

A catalogue record for this publication is available from the British Library

ISBN 978-1-009-49920-0 Hardback
ISBN 978-1-009-49918-7 Paperback
ISSN 2634-0763 (online)
ISSN 2634-0755 (print)

Cambridge University Press & Assessment has no responsibility for the persistence or accuracy of URLs for external or third-party internet websites referred to in this publication and does not guarantee that any content on such websites is, or will remain, accurate or appropriate.

For EU product safety concerns, contact us at Calle de José Abascal, 56, 1°, 28003 Madrid, Spain, or email eugpsr@cambridge.org

From Club to Commons

Enlargement, Reform and Sustainability in European Integration

Elements in Economics of European Integration

DOI: 10.1017/9781009499194
First published online: September 2025

Veronica Anghel
European University Institute

Erik Jones
European University Institute and Carnegie Europe

Author for correspondence: Veronica Anghel, veronica.anghel@eui.eu

Abstract: The Element identifies the logic of how the European Union (EU) has developed both in terms of the way the organization works and the way it has expanded to include new member states. It combines insights from the economic theories related to clubs and common-pool resources. The argument is that the EU may have started as a club, where members agreed to loose arrangements to generate and govern non-rivalrous goods from which only they could benefit, but it quickly evolved into a system of common-pool resources, where members have to manage rivalrous goods, the access to which cannot easily be refused to outsiders. That evolution was necessary to avoid the depletion of the goods EU member states depend on. The argument is illustrated through the evolution of the single market, the single currency, the single financial space, and security. This title is also available as Open Access on Cambridge Core.

Keywords: European integration, club theory, European security, EU enlargement, common-resource pool

© Veronica Anghel and Erik Jones 2025

ISBNs: 9781009499200 (HB), 9781009499187 (PB), 9781009499194 (OC)
ISSNs: 2634-0763 (online), 2634-0755 (print)

Contents

1 Introduction   1

2 Club Theory, Theories of Economic Goods and European Integration   7

3 The Implications of Accessing Attractive Goods   20

4 The Evolution of EU Economic Governance   37

5 The European Union as a Security Provider   53

6 Conclusion   66

List of Abbreviations   71

References   72

1 Introduction

Russia launched a full-scale invasion of Ukraine on February 24, 2022. In response, the European Union activated an accelerated enlargement process for Ukraine, Moldova, and Georgia that demonstrated the bloc's concerns about its own security as well as its commitment to stand up to Russia's renewed threats (European Council 2022, 2023). In 2023, the EU agreed to open accession talks with Ukraine and Moldova, a first step to integrate those countries into the single market and promote business cooperation. And in June 2024, the EU started accession negotiations.

This determination from the European Council to support Ukraine's war effort and European path raises important questions. How does the enlargement of the European Union contribute to fundamental European interests, such as collective European security or the collective prosperity of existing EU member states and citizens? How does a wider membership help the organization meet its institutional needs to increase its resilience and sustainability?

The EU also responded to Russia's full-scale invasion of Ukraine by triggering a major debate about reforming its institutions and governance arrangements. That debate gave rise to similar questions about how governance reform contributes to the security, prosperity, and resilience of the European Union. These are hardly new questions. The overlap of major debates about enlargement and institutional reform is not new either. The transformation and enlargement of the European Union go hand in hand.

We argue in this "Element" that there is a logic to how the European Union has developed both in terms of the way the organization works and the way it has expanded to include new member states.[1] That logic is consistent with the European Council's decision to extend a membership prospect to Ukraine, Moldova, Georgia, and the Western Balkans. The same logic also applies to the transformation of EU governance.

The European Union exists to produce and manage goods that are at the same time attractive to outsiders and prone to exhaustion or misuse. Economists and political scientists refer to these goods as common-pool resources. Such goods are highly vulnerable to the tragedy of the commons where individual incentives inevitably lead to collective self-harm. The only way to preserve such resources is through intrusive governance structures that impose discipline on

---

[1] This line of argument was first developed in Anghel and Jones (2025) with a narrow focus on attractive economic goods and broad focus on international organizations. This "Element" expands that argument by broadening the focus to include security as a good and deepening the concentration on the European Union.

all who have access. This is why the EU engages in institutional reform either in response to growing dysfunction or in reaction to external crisis.

At times, those governance structures can only work when they are also inclusive. This inclusiveness is critical not only to ensure that key actors have a stake in the European project and so accept the loss of sovereignty implied by intrusive governance arrangements but also that the EU as a whole can act with greater autonomy vis-à-vis the rest of the world. The European Union's push for enlargement – both historically, and after Russia's full-scale invasion of Ukraine – can be understood in that context.

1.1 The Economic Case

To make the economic case for our argument, we unpack notions connected to the attractiveness and exhaustion of the goods the EU generates, common-pool resources, and the tragedy of the commons. This requires a brief introduction to concepts from club theory (Buchanan 1965) and the theory of economic goods (Ostrom 1990; Ostrom et al. 1999), which we elaborate upon later in the "Element." A club is a voluntary association of actors deriving mutual benefits from sharing a good characterized by high excludability to outsiders, and low rivalry among members for the access of that good. The goods clubs administer are known as club goods (Sandler and Tschirhart 1980). Common-pool resources are defined by low excludability, and each actor's use of such resources subtracts benefits that others might enjoy (Ostrom 2008). Both club goods and common-pool resources differ from public goods. Public goods are found in those systems where it is most difficult to limit access, but one actor's use of the goods does not subtract from another's use.

Our argument is that the European Union has developed as a system of common-pool resources where it is increasingly difficult to exclude non-members from accessing the goods that it produces, and where the access of any one participant adds competition for (as well as potentially enhancing) the benefits available to others. This progression was a result of the success of the European project in attracting outsiders' economic activity – trade, money, investment, and migration – to the original member states (Stone-Sweet and Sandholtz 1998). The increasing openness was also a matter of choice as well as circumstance. At key points in the EU's history, European policymakers chose to provide access to goods across political, administrative, and sectoral boundaries to ensure efficient governance (Heritier 2002). In this sense, the European Union may have started as a club of six like-minded member states determined to build a common market so that they could benefit from greater trade with one another, but it quickly evolved into something much harder to manage in terms of access and competition, not only as that relates to the trade in goods and services but also with reference to the requirements for monetary and financial stability.

This new activity was vital to the economic performance of the member states, but it also created a series of related challenges to ensure that:

- non-state actors such as firms and individuals, based inside the member states, benefitted at least as much from the project as non-state actors from non-member states;
- non-state actors such as firms and individuals, based outside the member states, did not come in unlawfully or in some other way take advantage of the common market;
- the member states did not introduce policies that would take advantage of one another or in some other way undermine their common project; and,
- the common market not only functioned adequately but also continued to attract economic activity from abroad.

The volume of non-member non-state actors successfully drawn to the EU is a first telltale sign of the difficulty the EU has restricting access to the goods that it produces – what economists refer to as low excludability. The goods that the EU generated for its members were too attractive to keep away from outsiders, whether migrants, workers, refugees, businesses, or governments interested in accessing the benefits of the single market. This is an example of changing circumstances. Examples of how the EU decided to increase access to its goods to strengthen governance arrangements include the series of Trade and Cooperation Agreements signed with Central and Eastern Europe countries in the 1990s, or the European Neighborhood Policy launched in 2003. Such agreements were originally designed to avoid giving a formal membership prospect to countries on the borders of the European Union. That proved to be insufficient and so the EU opted for formal enlargement as a better alternative.

The competition or rivalry between multiple actors who want to access EU-generated goods further justifies the reclassification of the EU as being more like the administrator of common-pool resources than a club, in terms of economic theory. This is a second indicator. Each time the European Union or its predecessor organizations enlarged, competition within the internal market increased both for European participants and for those who came from outside. More importantly, European policymakers took deliberate decisions to encourage that increase in competition, first by lowering formal barriers to the trade in goods and services across countries and with the outside world, then by tackling non-tariff barriers, liberalizing capital flows, and fostering the free movement of individuals. At each step along the way, European policymakers were clear in articulating the ambition to make Europe more attractive and more dynamic, even if that meant existing firms or ways of doing business would lose out to new competitors.

A third revealing sign of the EU's transformation from a club to a system of common-pool resources lies in the evolution of the governance arrangements that underpin the EU. That transformation was necessary to allow the organization to continue to function in a sustainable manner. The EU pursued increased integration through closer management, a characteristic of regimes created to govern common-pool resources. EU member states increasingly exercise greater self-discipline to enforce the rules at home and multilateral surveillance to ensure they are enforced in other countries. Such arrangements do not necessarily require the expansion of formal membership of the European Union. But sometimes the best way to address these challenges involves inviting new governments to join and increase their stake in the sustainability of the EU project. That expansion of membership made running the organization more complicated, but it also brought in new ways to generate more of the needed shared resources, and it offered greater control over the firms and individuals of the new member states, and ultimately over the politics and international allegiances of those governments.

This story of the European Union's evolution from a club to a more complex arrangement for the administration of common-pool resources explains why the deepening and widening of the European project happened at the same time. The more national economies became tied to one another through the interaction of firms and individuals, the more policymakers at the national level needed to coordinate their actions with one another to prevent decisions taken in any one country or regulatory jurisdiction from conflicting with or thwarting actions in any other. Policymakers also needed to coordinate at the European level to respond more effectively to decisions taken elsewhere, like the United States or Japan. Formal enlargement is simply the most comprehensive way to coordinate with a government whose economy – firms and individuals – is already deeply engaged in European markets; it is also a tool to increase the weight and influence of Europe vis-à-vis other global actors.

The same incentives for policy coordination that work across national boundaries within the European Union operate between the EU and governments outside. This parallelism suggests why European institutions – including the budget – only tend to adapt to the requirements of a wider membership after the fact. The 1987 Single European Act was a response to increasing competition from U.S. and Japanese firms as well as to the enlargements that took place in 1973 (United Kingdom, Denmark, and Ireland), 1981 (Greece), and 1986 (Spain and Portugal). The 1992 Maastricht Treaty was primarily an instrument to promote monetary union while strengthening EU democracy. But it was also a response to German unification in 1990, which did not change the number of member states but certainly increased the size and composition of Germany and so changed how the member states interacted. The 1997 Amsterdam Treaty was at least partly a response to the enlargement to Austria, Finland, and Sweden in 1995. And the 2009 Lisbon Treaty was in many ways a delayed response to the 2004 and 2007 enlargement to the countries of Central and Eastern Europe.

The expansion of the European Union to Ukraine, Moldova, Georgia, and the Western Balkans makes sense, following this line of reasoning, if that is the best way to integrate the economic actors in those countries into the European Union's economy – by which we mean the single market, the single currency, and the single financial space – on a sustainable basis. It also makes sense if the alternative to enlargement is to lose control over the access that firms or individuals in those countries have to the goods that the EU produces or to watch the economies of those countries fail in ways that could undermine the prosperity of the European Union.

1.2 The Security Case

An alternative reading of how the EU developed to administer common-pool resources would be to consider whether the bulk of its activity focuses on generating and administering public goods. To explore this alternative, we trace how the EU manages what is often considered a public good: security (Kindleberger 1986). What we find is a pattern that looks very similar to that apparent in the case of the single market, the single currency, and the single financial space. In the case of security, the EU presents a higher degree of rivalry than we typically associate with public goods and less excludability than we would expect to find with club goods. This rivalry–exclusivity combination suggests that the EU as a security provider has evolved toward something that looks like the administrator of a common-pool resource – where one actor's consumption can subtract from another's and where actors outside the EU manage to access the EU's security without paying the cost of membership.

Enlargement to Ukraine (etc.) is part of a wider strategy to generate security for the European Union in a more sustainable manner. That strategy also includes a sweeping reform of European institutions and economic arrangements. This interpretation seems at odds with traditional conceptions of alliance politics. But the EU creates security in ways that typically garner less emphasis within a traditional military alliance. The EU exists to create economic interdependence through political integration. An important reason for creating that economic interdependence is to generate and preserve peace and security on the continent. In that sense, the EU has never fully been a civilian project. The European project was created with security in mind in the wake of the Second World War (Segers 2023). And it succeeded. That is why it won the Nobel Prize for Peace in 2012.

The mechanism for this security generation strategy can be explained in two ways. One explanation points to the need to reconcile ancient antagonists, such as Germany and France, France and the United Kingdom, the capitalist West and postcommunist East (Willis 1968; Vachudova 2005). The other is deterrence. If the EU embraces another government and makes itself dependent upon that country in important ways, the government of a third country should be deterred from risking the consequences of also harming the EU through an aggressive action. Here, it is useful to recall the EU's determination to expand to the Baltic States in the late 1990s (Kuus 2007). It is also worth considering the role the EU plays in the triangular relationship between Greece, Cyprus, and Türkiye. A third example is the impact of EU membership on relations between Britain and Ireland during the period they were both member states and after the British left the European Union.

The European Union can extend the prospect of membership to Ukraine as a security guarantee because doing so makes the EU vulnerable to any damage that Russia does to Ukraine. That integration of Ukraine gives all the more reason for the EU to push back against Russian aggression – and so adds credibility to bilateral security guarantees that Ukraine has with individual EU member states. Ukraine can embrace that notion of security because it hinges critically on the extent to which Ukrainian citizens and firms become embedded in the European single market, single currency, and single financial space. This combination is not easy to engineer, not least because of the strains further expansion of formal membership will place on European institutions. Nevertheless, the EU can accept that this arrangement requires significant institutional reforms that will be hard to accomplish, because it needs those reforms in any case given the extent to which Ukrainian (and Western Balkan) firms and individuals are already embedded in Europe. Significant institutional reform would be even more imperative for the promotion of European security if Ukraine were to fall to Russian aggression (Anghel 2025).

1.3 The Structure of the Argument

We develop this argument in five steps. Section 1 provides the theoretical foundations for our inquiry. We start with the literature on the economic theory of goods, which includes both a concern for the "tragedy of the commons" and the economic theory of club goods. We connect insights from these areas of inquiry to the economic theory underpinning regional integration in the

European context, particularly as it links the need for openness to the challenge of maintaining competitiveness. In that first section, we posit that the EU as it exists today functions as a system of common-pool resources rather than a club. Section 2 shows how the EU produces attractive goods and how the way outsiders access those goods contributes to but also runs alongside changes in governance arrangements and formal membership. Section 3 illustrates this club-to-pools evolution of the main economic goods that the EU produces: the single market, the single currency, and the single financial space. Section 4 illustrates the same transformation of the EU in how it generates security as a non-economic good. Section 5 concludes with policy implications that can be derived from this reconceptualization of the EU based on the underlying goods it manages. This conclusion brings us back to the current situation to show how our interpretation (or framing) of the EU as a system of common-pool resources can help us anticipate what is likely to come next.

This argument has important policy implications. By framing the EU as a system of common-pool resources, we accept concern that enlargement will bring increased congestion, heterogeneity, and rivalry over resources. But we are also able to offer solutions – or, perhaps better, ways to think about finding solutions – for how best to adapt governance structures to make those goods the EU creates more sustainable. And, in seeking to make the EU more resilient, widening and deepening are part of the same process.

2 Club Theory, Theories of Economic Goods and European Integration

Garrett Hardin (1968) wrote a controversial essay in *Science* about the incompatibility of a world of common resources and individual freedom or self-help. The reason for the contradiction, Hardin argued, is that individuals have incentives to overconsume or otherwise abuse the resources to which they have access. As a result, they inevitably reach a point where aggregate consumption (and waste) will overwhelm the production of the underlying resources. Worse, this is a problem with "no technical solution" (Hardin 1968: 1243). The only effective solutions are political. One is to limit access to some select few who can access the resource without overburdening it (Hardin 1968: 1245); another is to develop a system of governance based upon "mutual coercion, mutually agreed upon" as a means of ensuring that all those who have access do so responsibly (Hardin 1968: 1247). The first solution is to form a club, with the main question being how to defend the privilege of the few against those who are excluded. The other is to find some way to administer common resources that is sustainable in both political and technical terms.

Elinor Ostrom won the Nobel prize for her work theorizing and documenting the different ways societies organized themselves around mutually agreed upon mutual coercion to ensure the sustainability of common-pool resources (Ostrom 1990). While Ostrom developed this theory to evaluate the provision of public goods at the micro and local level, its insights traveled well beyond and became useful to those seeking to find solutions to manage international and global commons, including Ostrom herself (Keohane and Ostrom 1994; Ostrom et al. 1999; Vogler 2012; Buck 2017). Authors investigated the role of global, regional, and other international institutional arrangements in managing public goods (Keohane and Ostrom 1994; Sandler 2006). Such authors showed that actors who deal with common resource administration problems are not necessarily trapped in a "tragedy of the commons" but can in fact develop rules of cooperation to administer sustainably the goods they need and mediate discord in sharing the goods (Krasner 1983; Axelrod 1984; Haas et al. 1993). Indeed, the connections between international relations scholars who investigate modes to enhance cooperation among multiple self-interested actors, and scholars of common-pool resource administration should be numerous. From rules aimed at regulating farmers' rights to pasture, to those governing nations' access to water resources across state lines, to the global coordination of policies that permit the recovery of the earth's ozone layer, these are all collective action problems that may benefit from Ostrom-style solutions based on rules for efficient coordination.

And yet, despite the convergence between theories of economic governance that follow in Ostrom's legacy and theories of effective international regimes, most of the literature that seeks to understand world politics do not actively incorporate Ostrom's arguments (Keohane 2010). One of the reasons for this outcome is that Ostrom's insights are thought to apply to small-scale communities. Moreover, she primarily investigates the governance of goods that are produced by natural systems, such as forests and fisheries. The goods administered by voluntary groups of international actors that engage in collaborative activities, on the other hand, are not always material goods produced by nature. Security is one such example of a good that does not naturally exist; it must be created. This is what The North Atlantic Treaty Organization (NATO) produces and administers. Economic policy coordination is another example of a good that does not naturally exist; this is what is being produced by international bodies such as the G7. The single market is a good created by the members of the European Union that otherwise would not exist.

Most scholars choose to investigate how voluntary groups of actors, such as NATO, the G7, or the EU, administer the goods they create, using club theory and not Ostrom's rules for governing the commons (or, as she named them, common-pool resources). Since James Buchanan first introduced the theory of clubs in 1965, scholars have found his insights useful in myriad ways (Sandler and Tschirhart 1997). And they found applications derived from club theory in the study of "treaty formation, military alliances, wilderness areas, cities, roads, antibiotic use, the Internet, international organizations, and customs unions" (Sandler 2013: 266). Scholars also adapted the basic principles that derive from club theory even as they realized that pure club goods or pure public goods are not in fact common occurrences (Olson and Zeckhauser 1966; Sandler 1977, 1993; Sandler and Forbes 1980; Murdoch and Sandler 1984). We claim that modeling what such scholars may refer to as "impure" club goods, would be better served by Ostrom's work on governing common-pool resources.

This distinction between club goods, albeit impure, and common-pool resources is important in the context of the governance of the European Union, particularly as the organization has decided to undergo a process of enlargement that does not directly fit the size-optimization logic of how a club functions. EU membership is less a matter of privilege than a matter of "mutual coercion, mutually agreed upon." The 2022 revival of the European Union's enlargement process rekindled conversations on the trade-offs between "deepening" governance structures, generally defined as the rise in the scope and the level of European integration, and "widening," understood as the enlargement of the EU to new member states. Given the salience of this debate in previous phases of enlargement, we can rely on an extensive body of literature for insights into the interaction between the two phenomena. A literature review of the interaction between widening and deepening, however, reveals divergent and contradictory findings. We suggest that once we integrate insights from the theories of economic goods more consistently in our evaluations of the evolution of the European Union, we can identify the underlying reasons for this variance. These reasons go beyond the degree of purity of club goods and extend to the arrangements governing common-pool resources.

2.1 Widening versus Deepening

The major tension among those studies that pit widening against deepening is the result of a misclassification of the European Union as a club that generates club goods. Major problems of conceptualization dissipate once we identify the European Union as a system of common-pool resources, with important implications for choices regarding governance structures as well as membership. Moreover, once we notice that the European Union does not in fact operate as an exclusive club, we are also required to adapt what we mean by "widening." Many of the fundamental goods that the European Union generates are not exclusive to member states, questioning the "before and after" nature of enlargement.

The trade-off between widening and deepening received a lot of attention from observers seeking to understand European integration and to predict the future of the European Union (Kelemen et al. 2014a). Within this field of inquiry, the potential impact of widening on deepening has been the central concern of many EU scholars from the early phases of enlargement (Schmitter 1996; De Witte 2002; König and Bräuninger 2004; Marks 2011). These and other studies confirmed the trade-off between the two processes. Other studies, however, posit that widening and enlargement go hand in hand (Moravcsik and Vachudova 2003; Kopstein and Reilly 2006; Leuffen et al. 2022). Fewer studies would claim that, under certain conditions, widening can even lead to deepening (Kelemen et al. 2014b), or trigger pre-enlargement anticipatory deepening (van der Veen, 2014). Others directly confirmed that whatever the EU's adaptation strategies, widening had no impact on specific dimensions of EU coordination such as the EU's decision capacity (Toshkov 2017) or party cohesion and interparty coalitions (Hix and Noury 2009).

Despite their conflicting outcomes, such studies agree that the growing heterogeneity of EU members warrants close attention. Many even take issue with the rationalist club perspective of analyzing enlargement, showing that including states from Central and Eastern Europe in the early 2000s does not follow a club-size-optimization approach, raising questions of identity-building that go beyond calculating the trade-off "between the costs of congestion, administration, and decision making caused by expansion and the opportunity costs of exclusion" (Schimmelfennig 2001: 165). Figures 1 and 2 give an illustration of the heterogeneity that EU structures should accommodate in a future enlargement. Current candidate states differ widely across basic metrics such as population size and income per capita. Studies show how the EU reforms its governance structures to respond to changes brought about by heterogeneity, either by enacting "differentiated integration" (Schimmelfennig et al. 2015) or through pre-enlargement anticipatory deepening (van der Veen 2014). Occasionally, studies also signal that the governance changes that the EU enacts are incomplete and may not be fit for purpose in the long run (Jones 2018). The issue that such views do not address – and which is central to our argument – is that the EU is constantly under pressure to deepen and thus change its governing structures to organize collective action, even if formal widening does not happen.

Using insights from the economic theory of goods, we identify a connection between widening and deepening that eliminates some of the tensions in existing explanations of what the EU is and how it functions and accounts for the

Figure 1 Heterogeneity in terms of income

Source: IMF.

Figure 2 Heterogeneity in terms of population size

Source: IMF.

complex dynamics that are required by its governing structures. We claim that the goods that the EU provides are in fact common-pool resources where the EU must organize collective action to ensure their sustainability.

Part of the analytical challenge stems from the notion of excludability and access. While scholars may debate the meaning of deepening (Börzel 2005), what widening means has been uncontroversial in literature. This consensus on widening confuses access to the goods the European Union produces with formal membership. In important ways, even non-member states benefit from access through trade, investment, tourism, migration, student exchanges, and a host of other mechanisms. Some of that access is by circumstance, as through the development of global value chains. But much of that access is decided by EU policymakers through trade agreements or other forms of partnership with governments abroad. As a result, it is necessary to pay more attention to how non-member states access the goods that the EU has to offer, increasing not only the EU's heterogeneity but also the rivalry over the attractive goods that the EU provides. Such attention does not deny the huge benefits that come from having individuals and firms from outside the EU access the goods the EU produces. On the contrary, they make important contributions to the quality (variety, innovation, etc.) of European economic life. The point we underscore is that the advantages of access also create forms of rivalry that need to be managed.

In the next section, we explain how the EU transitioned from being a club to being a system of common-pool resources – with or without the formal decision to enlarge its membership. This insight raises a new set of questions related to the EU's necessary governance structures adaptation.

Our proposal to redefine the EU through the evolution of the common-pool resources it administers cuts across the different theories of European integration that focus attention on the empowerment of some EU actors and institutions through different procedures and at different points in time. For decades, scholars of European integration have engaged in debates on the locus of agency for European integration (Hooghe and Marks 2019). Those debates mostly pit supranationalism (with emphasis on the European Commission) against intergovernmentalism (where the focus lies on national governments whether within the European Council and the Council of the European Union, or with reference to domestic politics and less formal means for interest intermediation). These theoretical approaches to European integration have left many wishing for more substantive and methodological pluralism (Schmidt 2024).

In the theoretical framework we propose, answering who drives European integration is secondary to defining the real nature of the goods the EU needs to administer in what could be a plurality of ways. Through a different path, the theory of multilevel governance comes closest to the governance implications of our own analysis (Hooghe and Marks 2010). Multilevel governance theory already opens the way for scholars to enquire into the utility of another Ostrom concept for governance arrangements, namely the perspective of "polycentricity" (van Zeben 2019). Although we do not focus on polycentricity in this short "Element," we provide the basis for understanding how giving power and autonomy to many (instead of either ... or) local, national, and supranational entities, the European Union is more likely to avoid the depletion of its common-pool resources. Mutual coercion, mutually agreed upon extends vertically as well as horizontally. Again, widening and deepening are part of the same process.

2.2 Not a Club

That link between widening and deepening is harder to make within an analytical framing – like a "club" – that focuses on selective membership. And yet most scholars studying the European Union usually agree that it is a type of select club, even if they regard it as a unique kind of polity in the making (Ahrens et al. 2005). This tendency is shared across the study of international organizations more generally. The most advanced models for analysis that perceive most international organizations as clubs stretch to accommodate arrangements that vary from international organizations with ample size, such as the United Nations or the World Bank, to regional organizations, such as the EU or Mercosur. The goods that these organizations manage include peacekeeping, international finance, the environment, health, trade, human rights, criminal justice, and so on. Regional organizations are even more club-like insofar as they do not aspire to universal or encompassing membership. Instead, they should seek to achieve a kind of size-optimization that brings them closer to how economic theory defines a club.

That normative "should" does not hold in practice. Regional organizations do aspire to some level of exclusivity (Larsen 2021). Nevertheless, they create dynamics that make exclusivity hard to maintain, leading scholars to raise questions on the completeness of their club-like features (Sandler 1982; Brummer 2008). EU scholars in particular have shown that the EU does not always put size-optimization first when it decides to enlarge in terms of formal membership (Schimmelfennig 2001; Schimmelfennig and Sedelmeier 2002). Moreover, according to economic theories of integration, the goods regional organizations provide attract the attention of non-member non-state actors like firms, NGOs, or civil society organizations, lowering their high excludability potential even further (Mattli 1999; Higgott et al. 2000; Cowles 2003).

These non-state actors from non-member states seek to access the attractive goods that international organizations, such as the EU, produce (Stone Sweet and Sandholtz 1998). They also seek to influence how the goods are produced and how that production is managed. This dynamic extends the reach of the organization beyond its original member states. It also creates incentives for non-member state governments to associate with or even join the organization so that they can gain formal access to the privileges of membership; and it creates incentives for existing member states to open their doors to new participants in order to share the costs of governance arrangements from which these non-member states already benefit through the (informal or formal) participation of non-state actors (Hofmann et al. 2023).

These economic theories of integration do not tell us what happens to the organization that produces or administers such attractive goods as it becomes more open to outside actors and when it decides to enlarge or strengthen its governance arrangements. This is where we focus our attention. It is also where insights from the economic theory of clubs and goods become relevant to our research question. Some of this material covers ground that is already suggested in the introduction and yet it is useful to rehearse that material here to strengthen the link between the goods that are produced and the governance arrangements they require.

The economic theory of goods encompasses a set of four ideal types constructed out of two dimensions – excludability and rivalry (or subtractability) (Buchanan 1965; Ostrom 2003). Table 1 shows the ideal types of goods. These goods can be excludable or not excludable, meaning it is or is not easy to prevent external actors from accessing or benefiting from the goods. Any access to the goods can be rivalrous (or subtractable), meaning one actor's consumption of the good either takes away from its availability to others or it does not (Ostrom 2005). Goods that are excludable and subtractable are private while goods that are neither excludable nor subtractable are public. The illustrations are straightforward. A single apple is a private good because whoever has it can eat it and then no one else gets it; fresh air outdoors is a public good because someone breathing cannot stop

Table 1 Ideal typical economic goods

	Rivalrous	**Non-rivalrous**
Excludable	Private	Club
Non-excludable	Common-pool resource	Public

others from breathing and yet one's breath of fresh air does not deprive anyone else from breathing.

The mixed categories are more complicated to untangle. Goods that are excludable and yet non-rivalrous are club goods; and goods that are not excludable and yet rivalrous (or subtractable) are common-pool resources. Subscription video streaming is an example of a club good, insofar as adding more paying subscribers does not subtract from any other member's access to the good.[2] By contrast, a fishery in a river might be a common-pool resource because the people who live nearby may need to catch fish for food or business (which makes it hard to exclude them from access) and yet the fish consumed by one person is no longer available to the rest.

The traditional typology in Table 1 also suggests the governance arrangements attached to each of these goods (Ostrom 2005). The enforcement of private property rights is necessary to have private goods. A private good is excludable because the law (or some generally accepted rule) so dictates, and it is subtractable (or rivalrous) because whoever holds it has the chance to consume it. Similarly, public goods need to be provided by otherwise resourced entities who also defend the good against privatization. Public goods create positive externalities from which all can benefit without detracting from someone else's ability to enjoy that good. Governance arrangements for public goods require the protection of that good against those who might find ways to restrict access and so keep the benefits to themselves (Cornes and Sandler 2012). Those governance arrangements include boundary rules to define who should contribute to the production of the goods and how, but those rules cannot prevent actors from benefitting from the good once it is provided.

Club goods need to be generated and efficiently managed by ensuring that the marginal benefits of club membership outweigh the marginal costs of access. This definition goes beyond identifying a club as any kind of limited membership organization. In addition to having a selective membership, understood in this way, the club is a governance structure specifically designed to ensure a positive cost-benefit ratio for all members (Buchanan 1965; Sandler and Tschirhart 1980). As a result, the literature on club goods focuses on congestion and optimal sizing – as the good attracts traffic or the club grows, the resulting

---

[2] A streaming platform is an odd sort of club because – as a business model – such a platform shows increasing returns to scale, particularly in an age when the costs associated with personal computers or other networked appliances, high-speed connectivity, memory, and computational time are very low. Once we begin to reckon with the negative externalities associated with the energy and resources consumed supporting such a digital environment, however, we may take a different view (Coyle 2021).

congestion lowers the relative benefits. A larger group also promotes more diversity and creates greater opportunities for freeriding (Olson 1965). Hence the club relies on boundary rules to determine who can access the good as well as who contributes to its production and how they contribute.

2.3 A System of Common-Pool Resources

A common-pool resource needs even more stringent management to avoid exhaustion. Common-pool resources are essential both to those who have access and to those who do not, and the common-pool resource as a system has only limited productive capacity and so can be overrun by excessive demand. Like a club, the governance arrangement for a common-pool resource necessarily needs to restrict access and creates three kinds of goods – rights, roles, and substantive goods (Viola 2020). Unlike a club, however, the effort required to exclude those who want to access the common-pool good and to control those who have access is considerably greater. The logic of collective action surrounding a common-pool resource leads to overconsumption by individual members and the collapse of the resource if it is not appropriately managed. The challenge for any governance arrangement of common-pool resources is to internalize negative externalities insofar as they force everyone with access to appreciate the consequences of their own actions both for themselves and for the group (Ostrom 1990, 2005).

This notion of negative externalities is important for the argument insofar as it lumps together the many undesirable or unintended consequences of access to or consumption of a good that we do not capture (and hence are external to) parsimonious economic models for supply and demand. Some of these factors derive from congestion, heterogeneity, and freeriding in a relatively straightforward fashion. Other negative externalities relate to waste – think elephant tusks, rhino horns, and shark-fin soup, as well as various forms of pollution, including the destruction of natural habitats. Still others relate to the operation of complex systems dynamics, like the way social media algorithms focused on "clicks" might increase political polarization among adults and psychological distress among adolescents. The point to underscore is that these negative externalities are not the classical forms of "spillover" captured in European integration theories related to popular allegiance (Haas 1968), policy effectiveness (Schmitter 1969), or supranational governance (Stone-Sweet and Sandholz 1997, 1999). Instead, they are discrete problems that affect the sustainability of any productive system (Meadows 2015).

The governance structures illustrated in Table 2 provide a useful framework for analyzing international organizations like the European Union in their

Table 2 Governance arrangements underlying ideal typical economic goods

	Rivalrous	Non-rivalrous
Excludable	Recognition and enforcement of private property rights	Management to ensure marginal benefits outweigh marginal costs
Non-excludable	Organizing collective action to internalize negative externalities	Organizing collective action to generate positive externalities

capacity as administrators of economic goods. The governance arrangement and the type of good they provide are interconnected. This point is worth underscoring to focus attention on the substantive goods generated by the European Union and on the dynamic character of governance structures within such an international organization as they evolve in response to the nature of the goods they produce or manage. As contemporary theories of international organizations progressively delve into mapping complex interactions, the recognition of an organization's adaptive governance dynamics through the lens of the goods it administers assumes heightened significance. This is particularly true for a polity in the making like the European Union.

This notion of functional adaptation is implicit in the modern debate on international organizations – not as the only source of institutional change, but as one among several. For example, scholars have analyzed the connection that creates significant tension along the axis that runs diagonally from private goods to public goods. Proponents of the international economic order set up in the post-Second World War period argued that the protection of private property is necessary to generate the positive externalities associated with market exchange (Ruggie 1982); critics of that arrangement have argued that such a regime is not only exclusive but also inherently inequitable (or subtractive) and posited that any such arrangement should be viewed as a form of expropriation of global economic activity to create a private good for those who are already wealthy (Prebisch 1962).

Following this line of argument, the global economy is a public good from which no country should be excluded (Myrdal 1956). Yet scholars of international organizations did not observe this kind of democratization entailed by the progression from private goods to public goods at the global level. Instead, international organizations are seen to attempt to reinforce club-like governance arrangements in the form of selective membership groups within international organizations that preserve the power of specific countries (Viola 2020; Pelle et al. 2021).

This argument about the reinforcement of privilege through the formation of "clubs within clubs" does not distinguish between a selective membership group that produces club goods and a selective membership group that manages common-pool resources. Nevertheless, the movement along the axis that runs diagonally from club goods to common-pool resources has received considerably less (if any) attention within the scholarship that focuses on international organizations.

This gap also applies to the study of the European Union. Students of economic clubs do not look at those organizations as evolving into the administrators of common-pool resources; their assumption is that the members will either stop any growth as the organization approaches the optimal size or leave the club to set up a parallel organization that offers a better cost-benefit ratio for its membership (Buchanan 1965). When noticing decreasing excludability in the administration of club goods, scholars working with the economic theory of goods are rather inclined to see these as instances of clubs "producing impure public goods" (Cornes and Sandler 1994: 255).

2.4 Changing Governance

By tracing when an international organization like the European Union moves from producing club goods to managing common-pool resources we highlight changes in the governance arrangements of selective membership international organizations as they expand.

Building on economic theories of integration and the theory of economic goods highlighted earlier, we identify three (individually) insufficient but (collectively) necessary conditions to predict a shift from an organization that administers or produces club goods to one that manages a system of common-pool resources:

1. The club's *exclusivity diminishes* as outsiders access the good (or goods) that the organization produces. This insight comes from the literature on regional integration.
2. *Rivalry increases* as competition for access and influence over the good (or goods) grows with more participants. This insight comes from the economic theory of goods.
3. *Governance arrangements tighten* to address issues related to heterogeneity, congestion, and freeriding. This insight comes from the new institutional economics tradition.

When these three elements come together, the experience of being a member state changes fundamentally because the governance arrangements impose greater responsibility for self-discipline and multilateral surveillance to protect the system that produces the underlying substantive good. This is the "mutual coercion, mutually agreed upon" that we draw from Hardin (1968) and that has been documented extensively by Ostrom (1990, 2005). Moreover, it is the governance challenge that lies at the heart of efforts to manage negative externalities as these are broadly captured in the literature on complex systems dynamics (Meadows 2015), which is the wider theoretical context within which Ostrom was working. As that literature underscores, the risk is not simply that some member states will lose privilege or status relative to others; it is more fundamentally functional. Where members rebel against this greater discipline, the underlying productive system that generates common-pool resources is vulnerable to collapse.[3]

The next section illustrates the mechanisms through which the European Union's exclusivity is challenged by non-member non-state actors. We also show how increased access to EU goods increases the rivalry among member states.

3 The Implications of Accessing Attractive Goods

The goods that the EU produces are meant to be attractive to people, and not just to governments or states. And once you put people at the center of any conversation about enlargement, the picture changes significantly. People exercise agency as individuals, through private forms of collective action, and through public institutions. For much of our argument, we focus on individuals, firms, and states, but we could – and do – expand the analysis to include other forms of civil society and international organizations. Any analysis of the European Union as a club-like arrangement should take these other forms of agency into consideration when trying to understand the "exclusivity" of the European Union because actors outside the EU can gain access to the goods that the European Union produces in different ways.

These multiple forms of agency are central to our argument about how the attractive nature of the goods that the European Union produces – coupled with the success that the EU has in producing those goods and policy decisions to attract business, investment, human capital, and tourism to Europe – can make access to these goods less exclusive and increasingly rivalrous (or subtractive) over time. In turn, the European Union responds by finding ways to structure cooperation among public institutions – mostly states – both inside and outside the EU to minimize the negative effects associated with that increasing access as a means of ensuring that the goods it produces remain attractive.

---

[3] Francis Gavin (2023) refers to this dynamic as the "problems of plenty."

3.1 Agency, Access, and Implications

This section illustrates that dynamic by separating out the different kinds of agency involved. The first two columns of Table 3 suggest different ways non-member non-state actors such as people and firms access the basic goods that the European Union produces, such as the single market, the single currency, the single financial space, and security. The third column introduces different arenas (forums, institutions, and agreements) that non-member state actors use to access the same EU goods. For example, the EU uses governance structures such as the Schengen Area or the European Committee for Standardization (CEN) and the European Committee for Electrotechnical Standardization (CENELEC), to engage with public authorities both inside and outside the European Union to address the challenges that increasing access of firms and people to European goods can create. Formal enlargement of the European Union to bring in new member states is essentially the strongest form of public-sector engagement across all goods.

Table 4 introduces the (potential) negative externalities that arise from increasing access to European goods in terms of heterogeneity, congestion, and freeriding,

Table 3 Changes in exclusivity: From limited access to formal enlargement

	Non-member non-state actors		Non-member state actors
	People	*Firms*	
Single market	Immigrants, workers, and tourists	Non-financial manufacturing and services	Schengen Zone, the European Economic Area, Association Agreements, CEN, CENELEC
Single currency	Foreigners holding euros	Invoicing in euros	Swap arrangements
Single financial space	Cross-border investors	Cross-border financial services	Banking Union, Capital Markets Union
Security	Asylum seekers, refugees, people displaced by conflict	Financial and non-financial firms	European Peace Facility, Eastern Partnership, Neighborhood Policy

Table 4 Negative externalities or forms of rivalry resulting from suboptimal sizing

	Heterogeneity	Congestion	Freeriding
Single market	Inefficient and unpredictable	Increasing friction, fewer economies of scale	Rule breaking
Single currency	Liquidity risk	Control over money supply	Moral hazard
Single financial space	Opacity, uncertainty	Less efficient intermediation	Flight to safety, sudden stop
Security	Lower interoperability, lack of strategic direction	Increased redundancy	Fewer resources, inequitable burden-sharing

as they have an impact on the single market, the single currency, the single financial space, and European security. This table does not include all possible externalities. As mentioned previously, there are many undesirable or unintended consequences of access that need to be managed. But the table does focus attention on those externalities that are most closely anticipated in the economic theory of goods as part of the argument for optimal club sizing. Importantly, both forms of private access mentioned in Table 3 – by individuals and by firms (or other forms of collective agency) – increase the heterogeneity, congestion, and freeriding in Table 4. These are two of the challenges that the EU needs to work with public authorities both inside and outside the European Union to address.

The arenas for coordination in the third column of Table 3 are only part of the solution to the challenges associated with increasing access or decreasing exclusivity. The EU can manage the negative externalities from increased private access to its goods by engaging with public authorities outside the Union through various arrangements such as the European Economic Area (EEA) or different Association Agreements.

Formal enlargement of the EU to these states as full members is not obligatory. At a certain point, however, it may be more effective to construct a more encompassing form of engagement and avoid ad-hoc solutions for each form of interaction. Formal enlargement of the European Union to bring in new member states is just one more way of structuring public sector engagement to address the challenges raised by the increasingly attractive and less exclusive goods that the EU produces.

3.2 The Single Market

Consider private access to the single market. Individuals from outside Europe come to the European Union as tourists, but they also come for shorter or longer periods to study, work, and live. Many citizens of candidate countries often already live in the EU before the accession of their countries. In 2003, before these countries EU accession, there were 69,000 Polish nationals living in the United Kingdom[4] and more than 177,000 Romanians were living in Italy.[5] In 2023, according to the Turkish Ministry of Foreign Affairs, 5.5 million Turkish nationals lived in Western European countries.[6] In 2023, there were 27.3 million non-EU citizens officially living in the European Union.[7] Figure 3 shows the number of long-term non-EU immigrants entering each member state in 2022 alone.

In a similar way, non-EU firms come to buy and sell goods and services. In the first quarter of 2024, the EU imported just under €600 billion worth of goods and services and exported just under €700 billion.[8] Figure 4 shows that with the partial exception of Georgia and Türkiye, candidate countries are already well integrated in the EU's economy. The single market is very attractive.

But this access to the single market is not without challenges. Non-EU residents may increase the demand for public services such as healthcare, education, and social welfare, straining resources, especially if newcomers are not fully integrated into the labor market. Ensuring their effective integration into the labor market and society often requires significant investment in language training, education, and social programs. Integrating non-EU residents can also pose challenges to social cohesion, particularly if there are significant cultural or linguistic differences, potentially leading to social tensions or divisions.

Managing the entry and residence of non-EU nationals necessitates robust border control and security measures, which are also costly. The presence of non-EU residents can also lead to political tensions and debates over immigration policies, integration, and national identity, affecting domestic politics and influencing public opinion and policy decisions. Just under 1.3 million non-EU citizens were deported from the European Union in 2023, and another 119,000 were refused entry at the borders.[9]

---

[4] Office of National Statistics (www.ons.gov.uk/peoplepopulationandcommunity/populationandmigration/internationalmigration/articles/populationbycountryofbirthandnationalityreport/2015-09-27).
[5] ISTAT (https://demo.istat.it/app/?i=P03&a=2003).
[6] Turkish Ministry of Foreign Affairs (www.mfa.gov.tr/the-expatriate-turkish-citizens.en.mfa).
[7] Eurostat (https://ec.europa.eu/eurostat/statistics-explained/index.php?title=Migration_and_migrant_population_statistics).
[8] Eurostat (https://ec.europa.eu/eurostat/en/web/products-euro-indicators/w/2-09042024-bp).
[9] Eurostat (https://ec.europa.eu/eurostat/en/web/products-eurostat-news/w/ddn-20240506-1).

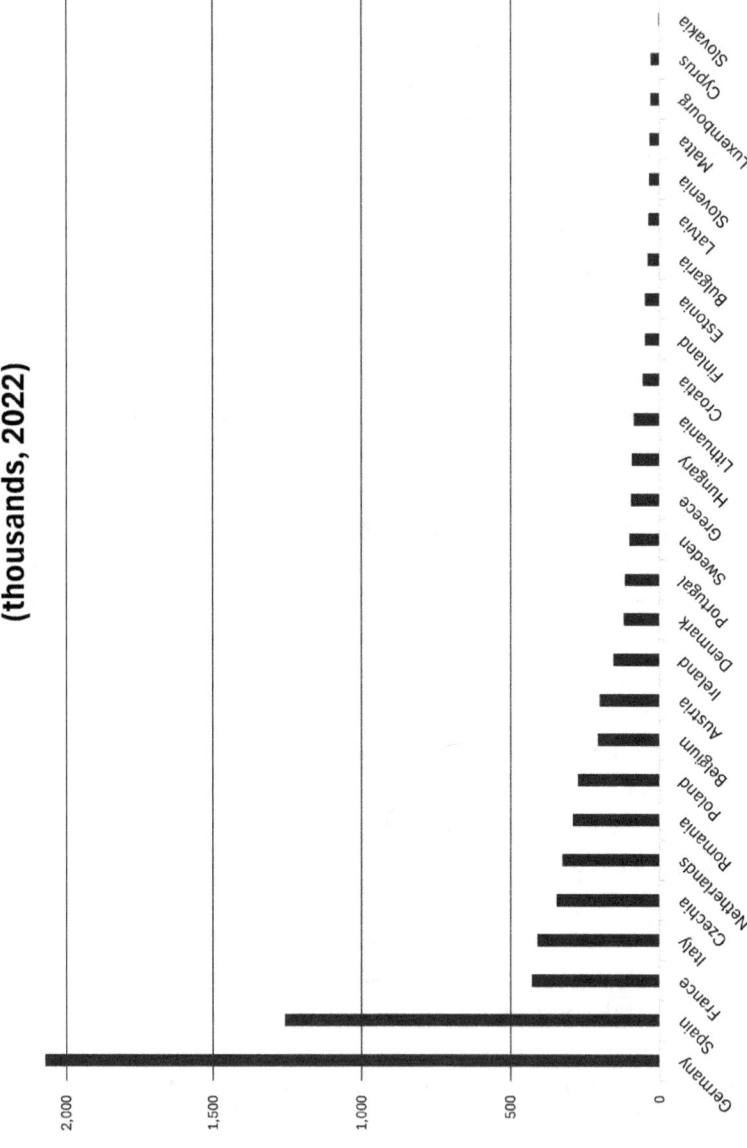

Figure 3 Exclusivity and immigration

Source: Eurostat.

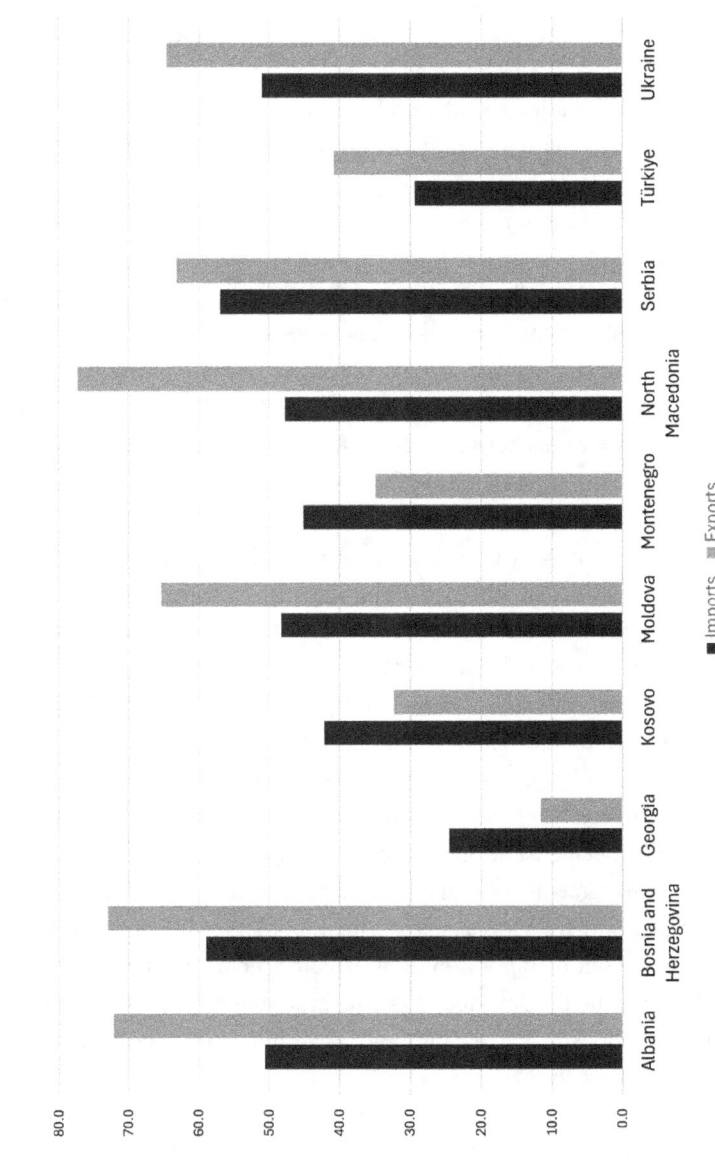

Figure 4 Exclusivity and firms

Source: IMF.

Ensuring the quality, functionality, environmental impact, labor protection, and intellectual property of manufacturing is another concern. As more people and firms from outside the EU enter the single market, European and national authorities need to invest ever greater effort to maintain access and fair competition for those already in the European Union without diminishing the single market's attractiveness (Young and Peterson 2014). These are the characteristics of a common-pool resource, not a club.

To address these challenges, the EU and its member states create new governance arrangements with public authorities both inside and outside the European Union. In the lightest form, they negotiate visa waivers, information-sharing agreements, trade arrangements, and international product standards. But they also create more intensive forms of cooperation like the Schengen Area and European standards bodies like CEN and CENELEC. They negotiate more complex agreements for governments to have deep and comprehensive trading relationships or to gain other forms of privileged access to the single market in exchange for sharing more information and for adopting European standards.

For example, all new member states starting with Greece in 1961 first signed an Association Agreement with the EU before fully joining the single market. Yet, for some countries, such as Türkiye, a candidate state which has had an Association Agreement with the EU since 1963, this arrangement looks like a more permanent fixture while membership is unlikely. Türkiye joined a customs union with the EU at the end of 1995 and it became a candidate country like any other a decade later, but its prospects for full membership are remote.

Türkiye is not the only exception. North Macedonia has benefitted from access to the single market based on an Association Agreement since 2001 and has been a candidate for membership alongside Türkiye, but it remains outside the European Union. In a different example, Norway, Iceland, Switzerland, and Liechtenstein have access to the single market through the EEA and they have agreements with the EU to participate in the Schengen Area, allowing for passport-free travel across their borders with other Schengen member states without being or aiming to become member states. While they are part of the EEA and the Schengen system, these countries do not have voting rights in EU institutions, which means they have limited influence over the rules and policies they must follow.

These countries and the EU must engage in bilateral and multilateral negotiations to manage their participation in Schengen-related matters, often requiring significant diplomatic resources. They must also deal with the economic impacts of aligning with EU policies and standards without having full access to the EU's decision-making processes. The governments of these countries have accepted this situation by choice. There is simply not enough popular support for joining the EU as a formal member state for them to go through the accession process. Norway and Switzerland have been invited to join, as has Iceland, but they have all declined the invitation – even though they accepted to make significant contributions to the finances of the European Union in exchange for the access they gained. These governments accept that they are not joining a club; even without becoming full EU members, they are being co-opted into the management of the single market as a European common-pool resource.

3.3 The Single Currency and the Single Financial Space

Access to the single currency and the single financial space works in a similar way. These illustrations are best presented together although the underlying goods – the single currency and the single financial space – are distinct. Foreigners can hold euros without ever entering the European Union, for example. Non-EU countries benefit from the Euro's stability, reduced transaction costs, enhanced trade opportunities, access to financial markets, and attractiveness to tourists and investors without directly contributing to the costs of maintaining the Euro. They avoid the financial burdens associated with Eurozone monetary policy, banking regulation, and financial stability mechanisms, which are borne by Eurozone members. This arrangement allows non-EU countries to leverage the advantages of the Euro while sidestepping the complexities and costs of its maintenance.

Sometimes this access to the EU is hard to manage. The popularity of €500 notes within organized crime syndicates is an example of how the euro has been used by people with access to the single currency even outside the European Union. By holding onto those €500 notes, organized crime syndicates have effectively made them inaccessible to EU citizens – which at least partly explains why the European Central Bank (ECB) decided to stop issuing those notes in 2016 (with effect from 2019).[10]

But organized crime is the exception rather than the rule. The main reason that individuals hold euros and firms write invoices in euros, is to travel to or do business in Europe. In turn, they get those euros from financial institutions that access European financial markets to facilitate trade or investment. Many of those financial institutions have links with or seek to compete with European financial firms that offer the same services. The ease of such cross-border currency transactions is part of what makes the single market attractive, and the more attractive the euro and European financial markets are, the more individuals and firms outside the EU will come to Europe to do business. As the data in Figure 5 shows, the euro is used for a large share of imports from and

---

[10] European Central Bank (www.ecb.europa.eu/press/pr/date/2016/html/pr160504.en.html).

28 *Economics of European Integration*

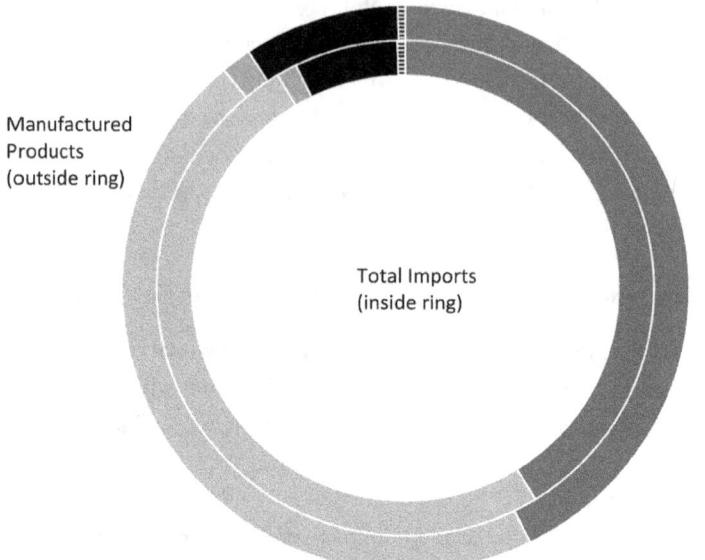

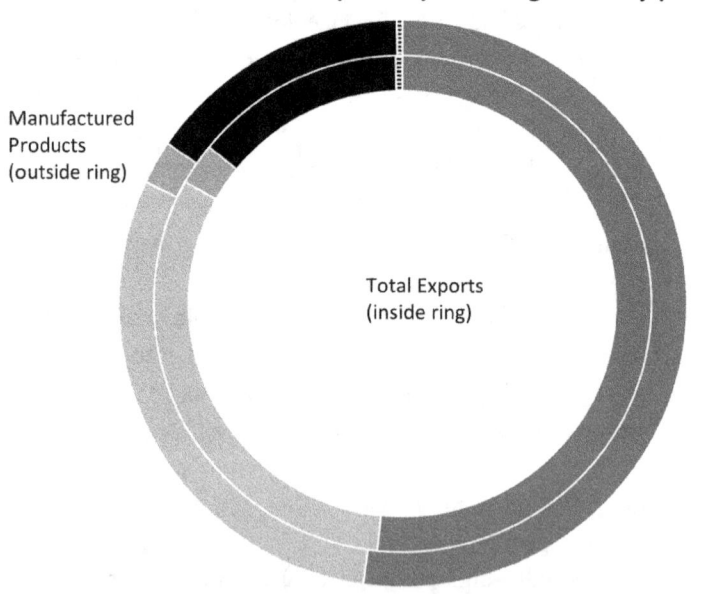

Figure 5 Exclusivity and currency use

Source: European Commission.

exports to markets outside the European Union, particularly in the trade of manufacturing goods.

Here again, there are challenges arising from this increasing access. Individuals holding too many euros outside the European Union create one set of problems. Individuals outside the EU who borrow in euros to finance their mortgages create another. The same is true for firms outside the EU that invoice in euros or rely on euros to make their payments. One of the main reasons that the governments of the Baltic States insisted on joining the euro in 2011 (Estonia), 2014 (Latvia), and 2015 (Lithuania) was to protect households with euro-denominated mortgages from a sudden devaluation of their national currencies during the crisis, for example (Dandashly and Verdun 2021). Such concerns are even more pressing for non-EU financial firms that compete in European financial markets.

Here the case of Iceland is illustrative (Benediktsdottir et al. 2011). Icelandic banks entered the euro area prior to the start of the financial crisis in 2007 to take deposits and lend money in euros. This activity generated significant profits for the banks in Iceland, but it exposed euro-area depositors (and any euro-area financial institutions that lent money to the Icelandic banks) to the risk that the firms and households that borrowed from the Icelandic banks would default, that Icelandic banks would not be able to return those euro-denominated deposits, and that any Icelandic deposit insurance scheme would be too small to bail the banks out. Worse, any effort by European depositors (and lenders) to pull their funds from the Icelandic banks would only trigger a run on the bank and a collapse in the value of the Icelandic kroner relative the euro – all but ensuring that those depositors (and lenders) would lose money. This is essentially what happened in 2008 (Thorhallsson and Kirby 2012).

The Icelandic case was an aberration insofar as the Icelandic banks were uniquely risky, but it was also representative of the dangers involved in the cross-border trade in financial services (De Grauwe 2010). Such cross-border activity always creates the risk that borrowers will not be able to meet their obligations, that national currencies will lose value suddenly against the euro, that financial firms will lose access to the markets, or that investors (both inside the EU and abroad) will suddenly liquidate their assets and spark a run from the euro to another currency like the dollar. These challenges were on full display during the global economic and financial crisis in 2008 and 2009, and they go a long way to explain why the crisis in Europe was so much deeper and longer than in other parts of the world (Jones 2015).

The EU sought to address these challenges through cooperation with governments outside the euro area and outside the European Union. It used central bank swap lines to help stabilize exchange rates and ensure the liquidity of firms and households. It also worked to coordinate with other governments in the deployment of unconventional monetary instruments, in the resolution of large financial institutions, and in the stabilization of specific asset classes (Jones 2009). Such action was particularly intensive within and around the European Union. As mentioned, governments in the Baltic States joined the euro area in response to the crisis.

The EU also created new forms of cooperation through the European Banking Union and the European Capital Markets Union in 2012 (Howarth and Quaglia 2016). As we develop in greater detail further, these were not club-like arrangements. They were much more demanding and intrusive in terms of their requirements both for banks and for regulators than the light-touch approach that accompanied the completion of the internal market and the liberalization of capital markets at the end of the 1980s (Alexander 2020). They also required substantial and controversial changes in the regulations surrounding investment protection and insolvency that were hard for national governments to implement.

Neither the Banking Union nor the Capital Markets Union have been fully introduced (Högenauer et al. 2023). The euro lost attractiveness during the crisis and so did European financial markets. That is why European leaders continue to insist on the need to redouble their efforts in strengthening these new governance arrangements (Piroska and Epstein 2023). It is why both Enrico Letta (2024) and Mario Draghi (2024) have put efforts to strengthen and reform financial market infrastructures at the center of their recommendations for improving the sustainability of the European project. And it explains why more governments – like Bulgaria – are striving to enter the euro area despite the rigorous demands associated with qualifying for euro-area membership, including the requirement to participate in the Banking Union and Capital Markets Union. The single currency and the single financial space are European common-pool resources as well.

3.4 The Security Good

The European Union does not provide the same kind of security in the same way as a military alliance like NATO. Nevertheless, as former Finnish President Sauli Niinistö (2024) stresses in his report to the European Commission, the European Union is a security provider. And the security that the European Union provides is very attractive to asylum seekers and those displaced by violent conflict outside the EU. More than 80,000 new asylum seekers apply to enter the European Union each month, primarily from war-torn countries like

Syria and Afghanistan.[11] The EU also provides temporary protection to 4.2 million people displaced by the war in Ukraine.[12] And the security the EU offers is also attractive to financial and non-financial firms based outside Europe that seek to protect their assets and intellectual property from their own governments. That attractiveness increases as countries on the borders of the European Union experience political turmoil or violent conflict, and as the governments of those countries turn away from the rule of law and toward more arbitrary forms of authoritarianism. Figure 6 shows the number of first-time asylum applicants for each European country according to the data for 2023.

This attractiveness of the European Union is a source of pride for Europeans. When more than one million migrants surged into Europe in 2015, the immediate reaction was one of solidarity (Wallaschek 2019). Migrants also add great strength to European society (Hansen 2021). But mass migration is a source of challenges. This is why we argue that it is useful to regard European security as a common-pool resource instead of as a public good. The more and more easily non-European citizens or firms come to the EU for their security, the more they raise complications for the European Union's ability to produce attractive goods. Some of these challenges relate directly to security. The influx of large movements of asylum seekers can complicate a government's ability to spot or track much smaller groups of terrorists. Other challenges relate to the functioning of the single market. Anyone locked out of employment for the time required to rule on requests for asylum may become a burden on society or a threat to law and order. To anticipate such possibilities for the great number of people fleeing the war in Ukraine, the EU Council triggered The Temporary Protection Directive for the first time to offer quick assistance and unlock benefits such as access to employment, social welfare and medical care. Figure 7 shows how many Ukrainians have been beneficiaries of this scheme in each EU member state as of April 2024.

The European Union's response in other cases has been to negotiate deals with third countries to hold and process potential asylum seekers. Since 2011 it has directed close to €10 billion to assist refugees and host communities in Türkiye.[13] The EU has also negotiated for the quick repatriation of asylum seekers whose claims are not accepted. Enlargement has played a role in managing these challenges as well. By pushing out the frontiers of the European Union and setting rigorous conditions for accessing the Schengen

---

[11] Eurostat (https://ec.europa.eu/eurostat/databrowser/view/tps00189/default/table?lang=en&category=t_migr.t_migr_asy).
[12] Eurostat (https://ec.europa.eu/eurostat/en/web/products-eurostat-news/w/ddn-20240508-2).
[13] European Commission (https://neighbourhood-enlargement.ec.europa.eu/enlargement-policy/turkiye/eu-support-refugees-turkiye_en)

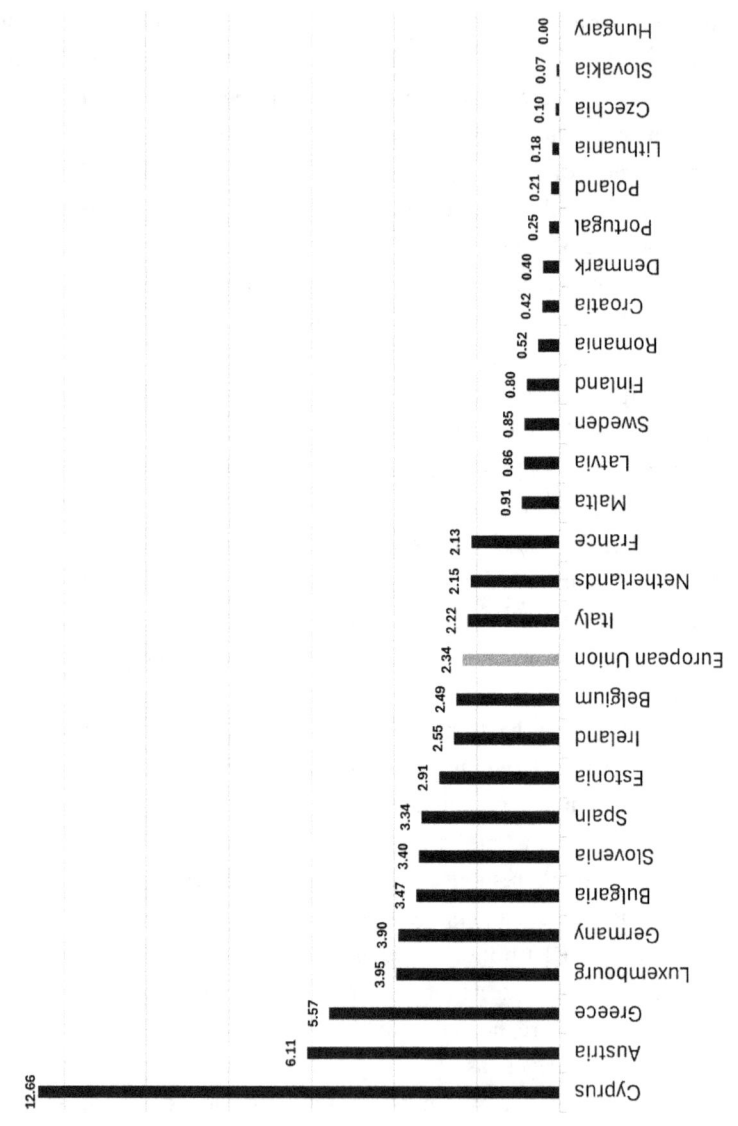

Figure 6 Exclusivity and human security

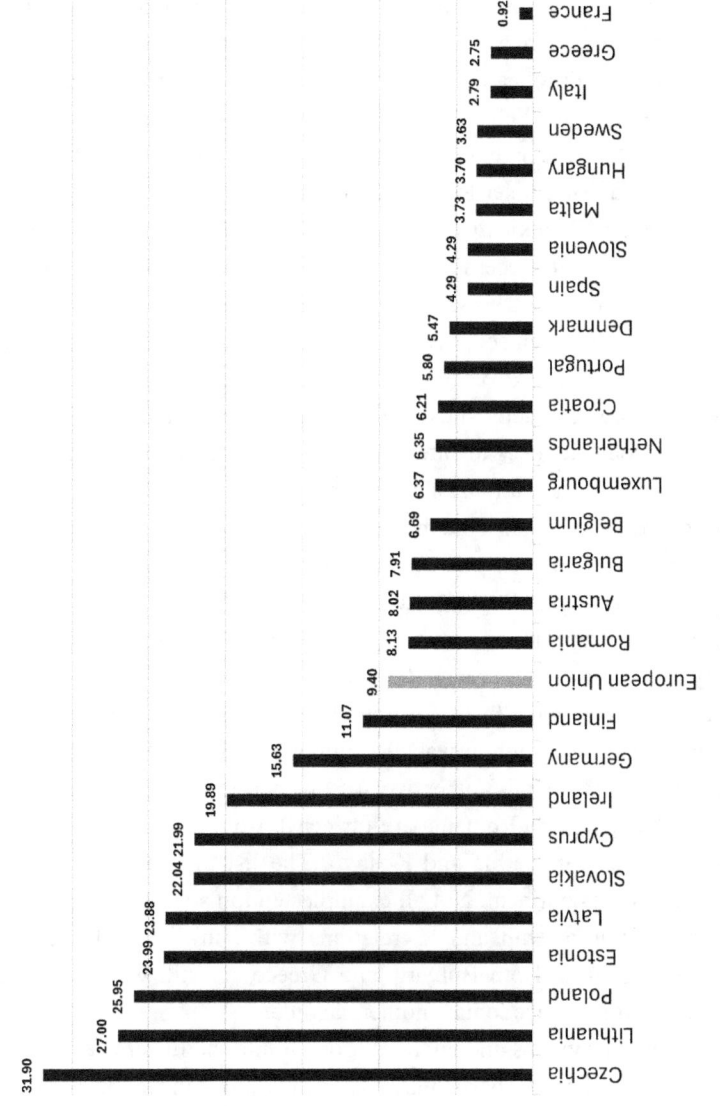

Figure 7 Exclusivity and temporary protection

Source: Eurostat.

arrangement, the European Union effectively co-opts governments into managing migration as a security consideration as well as a mechanism for protecting the single market (Favell and Hansen 2002).

The same kinds of strategies have been used to manage the migration of firms and their assets. Here the European Union faces challenges related to the provenance of any investments made for safekeeping and the potential influence that the owners of such assets might seek to exercise over member state governments and European institutions (Bauerle Danzman and Meunier 2023). The deposits made by Russian oligarchs into Cypriot banks is a good illustration, but so is the practice of some governments to allow the purchase of golden visas, requiring a set level of investment, and golden passports, with a higher price tag (Džankić 2018). Strengthening European control over such measures is increasingly necessary to ensure that the security Europe provides is not undermined by those who seek it.

The difference between security and other goods is that security also appertains directly to national governments as well as firms and individuals. In this way, the EU shares characteristics with more traditional military alliances like NATO. Some countries seek to enter the European Union to bolster the stability of their democratic institutions. This has been true since Greece, Spain, and Portugal joined in the 1980s. And the influence of Europe on these countries has been very positive. The historic enlargement to Central and Eastern Europe followed a similar logic (Anghel and Jones 2022).

Joining the European Union as part of a reconciliation process is also a security motivation. The Franco–German partnership is an obvious illustration (Willis 1968; Segers 2023). But the reconciliation between Germany and Poland or the Czech Republic was also important. So was the reconciliation between Slovenia and Italy, or between Slovenia and Croatia. Hungary and Slovakia or Hungary and Romania are further illustrations, as is the reconciliation process between Serbia and Kosovo. The list of examples is lengthy; Europe is a violent continent. Not all examples end in success. Cyprus did not unite prior to membership and its relations with Türkiye, still a candidate country, remain tense. Both Bulgaria and Greece are still working out their relations with North Macedonia, another candidate.

The variety of problems and interests brought into the EU creates an equally large variety of challenges, particularly when the European Union tries to assert its Common Foreign and Security Policy (CFSP) or its security and defense identity (Hofmann 2013). The problem is not just the various and overlapping red lines set out in relation to specific candidate countries, but also the historic relationships with other third countries like Germany's attachment to Russian hydrocarbons, Britain's special relationship with the United States, France and its former colonies in West Africa, Portugal and its Lusophone connections, or Greece and its connections with China. Most recently, the alignment of security interests of a member state such as Hungary or Slovakia with Russia as opposed to the European Union is one example of the difficulties to reign in a rogue state in the absence of a robust EU led foreign and security policy.

As it stands, the slate of EU candidate states would add to some of this heterogeneity on foreign policy alignment. Figure 8 shows the extent to which candidate states have aligned with the thirteen foreign policy declarations the EU issued from January 1st, 2023, to December 31st, 2023. In this period, the EU called on candidates, potential candidates, and partner countries to align with official statements made by the High Representative of the EU on issues ranging from packages of sanctions against Russia, measures against China or Iran, global human rights infringements or the proliferation and use of chemical weapons. The figure shows that most Western Balkan countries officially subscribe to EU foreign policy prompts, with the notable exception of Serbia, which mostly does not align with those declarations or with measures directed against Russia and China. That decision is primarily due to how Russia and China support Serbia's agenda on the independence of Kosovo, whereas the EU

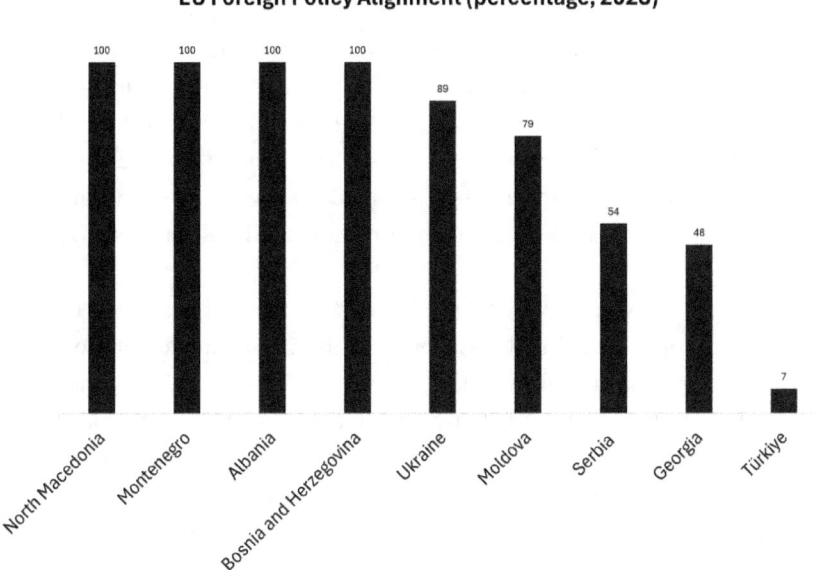

Figure 8 Heterogeneity and foreign policy
Source: Novaković and Plavšić (2024).

sees Kosovo as a country with an independent perspective of joining the EU. This will remain a thorny issue in the relationship between the EU and Serbia. Türkiye, although a NATO member, very rarely accepts to endorse EU official foreign policy.

In material terms, heterogeneity diminishes interoperability, reducing the EU's collective defense capabilities. The variety of interests and large number of national defense industries also create redundancy and inefficiencies in defense and law enforcement, complicating coordinated responses to threats. The European Union developed the Defense Technological and Industrial Base (EDTIB) to ensure deeper cooperation, avoid duplication, and underscore the interoperability of equipment. This endeavor is slow-paced, as member states remain predisposed to procuring weapons nationally or internationally, rather than accepting regional coordination (Wilkinson 2020).

Countries also freeride on European security. Neutrality is an example of freeriding in reference to the mutual defense clause of the EU enshrined in Art. 42.7 of the Lisbon Treaty. But freeriding can also result from excessive public indebtedness. Belgium and Italy are both NATO member states, but they have few resources to invest in collective security. This kind of freeriding results in inadequate resource allocation and inequitable burden-sharing, weakening collective efforts and leaving important gaps in defense and crisis response capabilities.

Such freeriding can be overcome. Following Russia's full-scale invasion of Ukraine, Denmark voted in a referendum to take part in EU security policy, giving up on its thirty-year opt-out; Sweden and Finland joined NATO. Nevertheless, the neutrality of countries such as Austria and Ireland – and the indebtedness of Belgium and Italy – will become increasingly problematic in view of the European Union's commitment to build a European Defense Union.

This potential explains why there is so much attention in current debates about the use of qualified majority voting in the CFSP, and about the use of common borrowing to finance collective defense (Youngs 2024). A large and diverse European Union suffers from significant negative externalities in constructing a CFSP or a European security and defense identity in much the same way that the single market, the single currency, and the single financial space struggle to manage the access given to individuals and firms from outside the European Union. But those security concerns would only get worse if governments were left out of the European project. Widening and deepening are both essential for the management of European security as a common-pool resource.

4 The Evolution of EU Economic Governance

The European Union produces goods that are attractive for people outside its borders, and it struggles to manage the consequences of allowing individuals, firms, and governments into the European Union. But that attractiveness is key to the European Union's success and so is access. Moreover, this tension has always existed in the European project. What started as a small club of six countries grew in size and complexity as a consequence. The initial club goods administered by the founding member states became increasingly rivalrous and less exclusive. The previous section explained why and how that shift in the nature of the club arrangement to a regime governing common-pool resources happened, highlighting the different ways people, firms, and governments outside the EU access the goods that the European Union produces, and then illustrating and underscoring the challenges that emerged as a result of that access. The purpose of this section is to show how the European project evolved over time in response to those challenges.

The focus of this section is on the three main economic goods that the European Union produces: the single market, the single currency, and the single financial space. In each case, it is possible to identify how member states start by administering the good according to club-like arrangements. Governments inside the European Community club agree to trade, stabilize exchange rates, and facilitate the movement of financial services and capital. Very quickly, however, the success of these initial ventures both in encouraging interaction within Europe and in attracting economic activity from abroad is exposed to the challenges of decreasing exclusivity and increasing rivalry. In turn, the member state governments begin to adapt European institutions, pass new regulations, launch new initiatives, and bring in new member states in an effort to tackle those challenges. The result is a more intrusive pattern of governance that relies more heavily on self-discipline and multilateral surveillance. What started as a club arrangement begins to look ever increasingly like the kind of arrangement required to administer common-pool resources.

The telltale signs of the shift from a club to a system of common-pool resources include changes in the governance arrangements to strengthen coordination across countries, increasing efforts to prevent policies in one member state from having a negative impact on all the rest, and heightened requirements (or opportunities) for member states to police one another for appropriate behavior. As we show this evolution, we are careful to keep track of the accession of new member states. We believe that EU enlargement is the result of similar dynamics that lead to the evolution of European governance structures: the more the individuals and firms of countries close to the European

Union become entangled in the goods that the European Union produces through migration, trade, investment, or finance, the easier and more attractive it becomes for existing EU member states to extend membership to the governments of those countries. Importantly, we do not argue that deepening causes formal enlargement or that formal enlargement causes deepening. The two processes are obviously related insofar as a larger membership requires different governance arrangements and a more complex organization can become more attractive to non-members (Grubel 2000). Whether governance reform or enlargement takes place is a political calculation reflecting many different incentives. Our point is that the same forces that result in reduced exclusivity and increased rivalry create incentives for governance reform and enlargement.

Via enlargement, the EU not only has more levers to strengthen policy coordination and so prevent policies in those countries from having a negative impact on existing member states, but it can also get the governments of those countries to contribute to the costs of managing the EU both directly and through multilateral surveillance. The challenge of enlargement is to adapt the institutions of the EU to the requirements of a wider membership. In this sense, enlargement is both a response to the need to administer the single market, the single currency, and the single financial space as a set of overlapping common-pool resources, and it is a reason for reforming the overarching governance arrangement.

For each section that follows, we provide a timeline that outlines parallel processes for each of our three cases – the single market, the single currency, and the single financial space. We present those timelines in Figures 9, 10, and 11. In each figure, we highlight three phases in the nature of the good: the club good phase, the shifting phase, and the common-pool resource phase. The outer edge of the chronology indicates the years when the European Community and the European Union enlarged to new member states and so is common to all three cases. The inner edge is different from one case to the next and points to specific milestones in the evolution of governance arrangements indicative of the transition from the management of a club good to the administration of a common-pool resource. This shift is not a sharp discontinuity, but a matter of degrees. We highlight the moment when the governance arrangements for each of the three club goods change to involve greater coordination, more attention to negative externalities, and heavier reliance on a mixture of self-discipline and multilateral surveillance. That shifting period ends when the governance arrangements for the respective good transform entirely to reflect more of the characteristics found in systems administering common-pool resources than club goods.

The narrative surrounding those graphics explains the judgments that we make. That narrative refers to enlargement as well as to changes in governance structures both as common responses to the same (or overlapping) sets of influences and as they interact with each other along the way.

4.1 The Single Market: From Liberalization to Rule of Law

The European Economic Community (EEC) that began with the Treaty of Rome in 1958 was a project of negative integration, removing tariffs and quotas that inhibited trade and then accompanying that with the development of a common external commercial policy. This is a club-like feature. France rejected efforts to broaden the membership of the club and pushed back against efforts to shift toward more positive forms of integration through the elaboration of common standards and the strengthening of internal governance arrangements (Silj 1967; Teasdale 2016). The most contentious element was the creation of a Common Agricultural Policy (CAP), which had characteristics closer to a common-pool resource that involved significant negative externalities and therefore also redistributive elements. But such tensions could be managed through the insistence on a national veto over matters of national interest through the 1966 Luxembourg compromise (Teasdale 1993).

From the outset, the success of the internal market lay in its capacity to foster trade and investment among European member states and between European member states and the outside world. That success in turn attracted the attention of individuals and firms from non-member states to focus on the opportunities created by the internal market. Hence, also from the outset, European governments worried that their own firms, investors, or workers would be put at a disadvantage by the increasing foreign presence in Europe. The debate that surrounded Jean-Jacques Servan-Schrieber's (1967) *Le Défi Américain* is among the most prominent examples, but there are many others across the decades. In this sense, we can draw a line that connects concerns about Eurosclerosis in the 1970s and early 1980s (Giersch 1985) with the Cecchini (1988) report on the costs of non-Europe in the late 1980s, the Delors (European Commission 1993) report on growth, competitiveness, and employment in the mid-1990s, the Kok (2004) report on the failure of the Lisbon strategy in the mid-2000s, the Brexit debate in the mid-2010s (Jones 2016), and Enrico Letta's (2024) report, *Much More than a Market*, or Mario Draghi's (2024) report on "competitiveness." In the previous section, we focused on the penetration of firms and individuals that reflects the attractiveness of the European project; here we focus on the European structural evolution that paralleled the reduction in exclusivity and increase in rivalry that was the result.

Figure 9 illustrates the evolution of the single market as driven by key documents and moments of enlargement. The documents are important to map the evolution of the governance arrangements, which move from negative integration in the form of elimination of tariffs and quotas to more positive integration in the form of common rules and standards. As this evolution takes place, European institutions begin to strengthen requirements for self-discipline and multilateral surveillance on the part of the member states. This transformation parallels the deepening of interdependence between Europe's internal market and markets outside Europe. It also parallels the expansion of formal

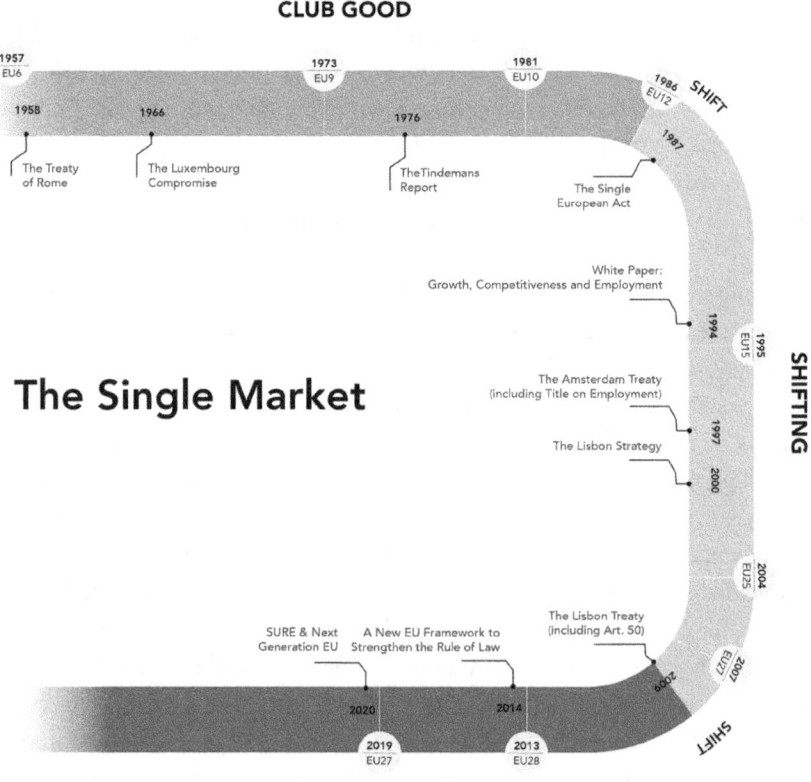

Figure 9 The evolution of the single market

Note: The figure highlights three phases in the evolution of the good. The outer edge marks the years of enlargement and the membership count. The inner edge features the main documents or decisions that confirm the governance arrangements specific to the nature of the good in that period.

membership. Moreover, these processes are interconnected insofar as greater independence, and a larger membership, require stronger rules for managing access to the single market.

The British, Danes, and Irish joined the European communities, at least in part, to become more competitive in an increasingly integrated global economy. The European Community admitted them to membership because that would make the internal market more attractive while at the same time providing greater control over trade and other forms of economic interdependence (Preston 1997; Kaiser and Elvert 2004). In turn, the first round of enlargement in 1973 placed immediate strains on existing governance arrangements. It also raised significant distributive conflicts among members and grievances about increasing heterogeneity and hence on the unequal access to club benefits. These were hardly the first distributive conflicts to arise. Much of the tension in the 1960s surrounding the CAP was distributive as well. But the conflicts that emerged in the 1970s were significant and they could not be resolved through the introduction of regional and structural funds as an instrument to reduce geographic disparities across the European Community. Nevertheless, the members of the European Community refused to abandon their club-like arrangement and embrace the more ambitious governance structures outlined in the 1976 Tindemans report (Mitchell 1976). As a result, those conflicts became an increasingly important constraint on the functioning of the institution. The British budgetary question was a major roadblock (Schramm 2024).

Further enlargement to Greece in 1981 and then to Spain and Portugal five years later exacerbated these complaints and required a change in the underlying governance arrangements to accommodate greater heterogeneity and to streamline decision-making processes (Preston 1997). The shift away from a club-like arrangement begins with the 1987 Single European Act. That treaty revision made it easier for the Council of Ministers to make decisions by qualified majority, but it also created a more robust framework for setting the rules for exchange between firms seeking to access the single market and those already inside (Pelkmans 1987). The addition of cohesion funds provided redistribution and aimed to ease tensions that resulted from increased rivalry. Nevertheless, these changes did not eliminate internal frictions and neither did they solve all the challenges associated with the functioning of the single market. The report by Tomasso Padoa-Schioppa (1987) made explicit reference to the need to adapt European institutions to the challenges resulting from a more heterogenous membership and the report by Paolo Cecchini (1988) underscored the continuing economic costs of non-Europe.

The problem was not simply a matter of resources. The further enlargement of the European Union in 1995 to small, wealthy countries from the Nordic and

Alpine regions made matters more complicated and not less. Although those countries were expected to become significant new net contributors, they also placed new demands on the governance arrangements to enhance their transparency, pushing the EU's shift away from the light-touch characteristics of a club-like arrangement even further (Miles 1995). Austria, Finland, and Sweden also required significant optouts and added congestion to decision-making.

Meanwhile, the completion of the internal market generated enthusiasm as a project and increased competition between European firms and multinationals headquartered outside Europe, and between European norms and regulations and the rules that govern production outside Europe. This sparked an important internal debate, and a 1994 European Commission White Paper about growth, competitiveness, and employment within the internal market (European Commission 1994). That debate extended across the 1990s to focus on the negative consequences of market integration between Europe and the outside world and the need for greater adaptability to the requirements for market competition within Europe. Importantly, this new European competitiveness should not result in reduced social protection or other forms of hardship. On the contrary, it was to strengthen Europe's potential to generate an inclusive labor market capable of ensuring well-remunerated, meaningful employment.

Another objective in the debate about European competitiveness was to ensure that national and (subnational) regional economies could adjust efficiently to macroeconomic shocks so that labor mobility across countries would not pose an undue burden on national politics. This additional requirement sparked significant skepticism within the economics community. Although economists regarded unemployment as primarily a local or regional phenomenon, they did not see a clear link between changes in European economic governance and the development of more efficient local factor markets (Viñals and Jimeno 1998). European policymakers nevertheless embraced the idea that the European Union could develop governance institutions that could have an important impact on labor market performance. The 1997 Amsterdam Treaty even included a new Title on Employment. The result was an extension of concern for relative labor market performance that grew through the accumulation of related reform processes – starting with labor markets and extending through macroeconomic dialogue to product markets – into the Lisbon Strategy (Radaelli 2003).

The Lisbon Strategy announced in March 2000 promised to strengthen the governance relationship by adding a new open method of coordination through which national governments could share best practice while at the same time encouraging one another to focus on making consistent progress. This arrangement was meant to be light touch and to run alongside the development of broad economic policy guidelines developed to shape national economic policies in the common interest. Instead, it multiplied the number of priorities to the point that it overwhelmed the management of the internal market. By the mid-term review that coincided with the 2004 enlargement to Central and Eastern Europe, European officials worried that the whole European social model was at stake (Kok 2004). The debate shifted to implementation and the adaptation of additional rules with the emphasis moving ever more clearly to multilateral surveillance and conditionality.

At the same time, the European Commission began to push a much stronger "beyond the border" agenda in trade negotiations that would extend new rules for accessing the internal market for firms (and governments) outside Europe (De Bièvre 2006; Young and Peterson 2014). It also began to use its regulatory authority internally and the attractiveness of its market externally to project regulatory requirements onto non-European firms even outside the framework of formal trade negotiations. Those outside firms would have to adopt European standards to access European markets (Damro 2012).

This shift deepened with the enlargement to Central and Eastern Europe in 2004 and 2007. The core of the formal enlargement process has always included an obligation for new members to approximate the *acquis communautaire*, or body of rules that make up the single market. For the enlargement to Central and Eastern Europe, however, the European Council established an explicit set of political criteria that extended to how the rules are made and enforced within the candidate countries. The "rule of law" could no longer be taken for granted, and so demonstration of the effectiveness of legal institutions became a major sticking point in the negotiations. It even became the justification for delaying the accession of Bulgaria and Romania, and it explains why those countries were brought in under special arrangements to ensure they continued to make progress in battling corruption and strengthening their judicial institutions (Vachudova 2005).

The final turning point from the single market as a club good to a common-pool resource came with the Lisbon Treaty in 2009. That treaty introduced greater protection for fundamental rights and gave the European Union full legal personality in dealing with matters of justice and home affairs. The Lisbon Treaty also made it possible for European institutions to enforce member state protection of the rule of law in all participating countries – provisions made stronger by the elaboration of a new EU framework in 2014 (European Commission 2014). And the Lisbon Treaty strengthened the abilities of the European Commission to ensure adequate protection of the environment. Finally, the Lisbon Treaty made it possible for member states to leave the

European Union, under Article 50. This provision reflected the reality that the organization many countries had joined had evolved into something with greater obligations for membership and more intrusive governance arrangements. Few expected that this provision would ever be activated.

But the governance requirements had changed. Within the context of the Lisbon Treaty, the balance of attention shifted away from market liberalization to addressing the negative externalities that arise as a result of the adoption of contradictory policies across member states. The most important of these contradictions concerns the maintenance of the rule of law. The single market is incompatible with a differentiated protection of the rule of law, as that leads to distortions in the protection of private property and the structure of market competition (Kelemen 2019). The difference between firms that pay the costs associated with their impact on the environment and those that do not also distorts the maintenance of the single market.

The EU dealt with such distortions not only by strengthening enforcement mechanisms, but also through the creation of new opportunities for redistribution and solidarity – like the SURE and Next Generation EU programs that were introduced during the Covid-19 pandemic (Buti and Fabbrini 2023). Such programs look like straightforward income transfers to member-state governments to support employment protection measures (SURE) or to promote the green and digital transition (NextGenEU), but they exist to offset imbalances across member states so that the relative weakness of some governments in protecting employment or the relative strength of others in financing transition do not undermine the functioning of the internal market. The programs also provide the European Commission with unprecedented powers to influence national policy-making and they create new opportunities (and obligations) for member state representatives to ensure any funds deployed in other countries are used responsibly and effectively. For many observers of European economic governance, this combination of measures constituted a "paradigm shift" in the economic governance of the single market because of the way it empowered the European Commission to help member state governments push through painful but necessary market structural reforms (Buti and Fabbrini 2023). From our perspective, what started as a club-good had taken on the appearance of a common-pool resource instead.

4.2 The Single Currency: From Monetary Stability to Macroeconomic Policy Coordination

A similar pattern can be found in the European project to broaden the zone of monetary stability (see Figure 10). Here again, we focus on the European

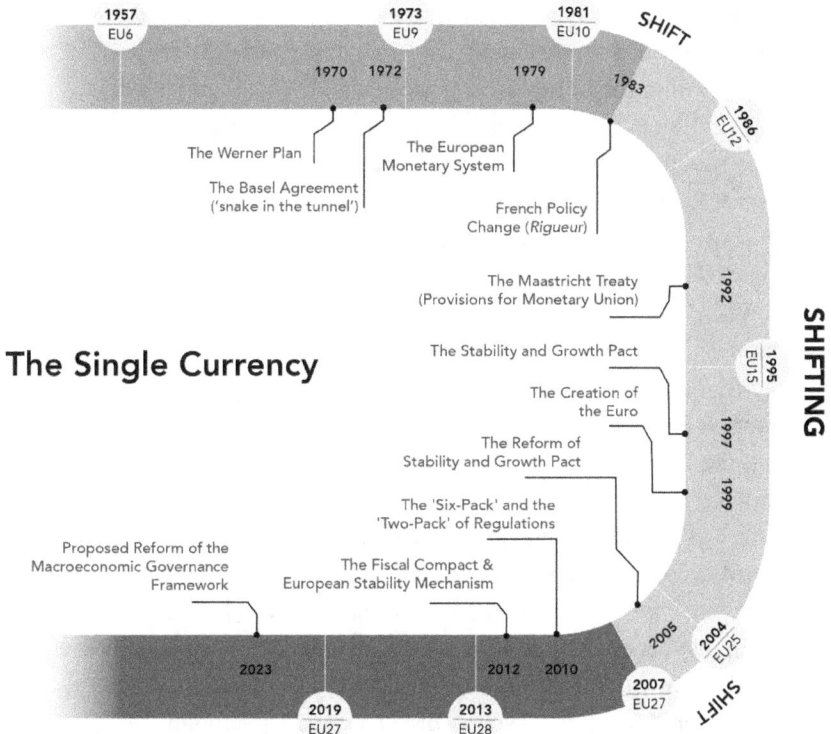

Figure 10 The creation of the single currency

Note: The figure highlights three phases in the evolution of the good. The outer edge marks the years of enlargement and the membership count. The inner edge features the main documents or decisions that confirm the governance arrangements specific to the nature of the good in that period.

response to the influence of non-state actors like firms and individuals. In this case, the most important are those who access European markets in ways that can distort the functioning of exchange rates. That European response started with efforts to construct a parallel exchange rate to strengthen the functioning of price supports within the CAP. Within the Bretton Woods System, the U.S. dollar already provided an anchor currency for multilateral exchange rates, and yet countries that participated in the CAP needed even more stability to achieve their agricultural objectives. The CAP operated on the basis of common price supports that became difficult to manage when there was volatility in the exchange rates between different currencies. The introduction of "green currencies" helped avoid excessive bilateral fluctuations within their commitments to the dollar exchange rate standard. Member states soon realized that a broader arrangement could also support the process of trade integration within the European Common Market (McNamara 1993).

In 1970, Europeans announced their intention to tighten their bilateral exchange rate fluctuations so that they could move jointly against the dollar. The Werner Plan outlined a club arrangement within the Bretton Woods System insofar as countries would coordinate their exchange rate policies to limit exchange rate divergences within Europe as they fluctuated relative to the dollar. When the Bretton Woods System collapsed, and new members joined the European Community, those efforts at joint coordination took on greater imperative. The goal shifted to replace the Bretton Woods arrangement rather than improve it (Tsoukalis 1977). Their efforts at stabilizing bilateral exchange rates via the 1972 Basel Agreement ended in failure. The European "snake" could not remain within the "tunnel" defined by permissible fluctuations against the dollar, and European governments could not hold the "snake" together in the absence of a dollar anchor. As the world moved toward more freely floating exchange rates, governments recognized that they would have to commit to more than just declaratory policy to produce monetary stability. That realization, admitted in the 1975 Marjolin report, led to the creation of a more ambitious European Monetary System (EMS) in 1979 (Marjolin 1975; Ludlow 1982). This transition from the "snake" to the EMS increased the size of the club again.

The EMS initially failed to stabilize exchange rates. During its first four years of operation, the exchange rate mechanism (ERM) was subject to repeated realignments. The problem remained that diverging domestic policies created powerful negative externalities for other members. The practice of competitive devaluations made that problem worse as governments took advantage of the stability already generated within the club-like arrangement by lowering the value of their domestic currency relative to the others and thereby gaining a relative cost advantage for their exports into the single market.

The 1983 French government's U-turn from Keynesian demand stimulus to more austerity (known at the time as *"rigueur"*) in its macroeconomic policy reflected the trade-offs entailed in seeking exchange rate stability. In our timeline, this moment marks the beginning of the shift in the process to create a single currency away from a club and toward something more like the administration of a common-pool resource. EU governments began to engage in concerted macroeconomic policy coordination and hardened the

EMS (McCarthy 1990). This shift away from a club-like arrangement was meant to manage rivalry among members and generate stability, as the focus for attention changed from who could participate in any arrangement to how much any participating country would have to exercise self-discipline in the conduct of macroeconomic policy and multilateral surveillance with respect to everyone else.

This requirement for greater discipline did not deter potential members. On the contrary, the success of the EMS attracted new participants. Italy narrowed its fluctuation bands, and the United Kingdom formally joined the ERM. Such coordination placed increasing constraints on national governments even as it lent credibility to domestic monetary policymakers (Giavazzi and Pagano 1988). And, while the political commitment to monetary stability found credibility in the markets, the potential for destabilizing speculation against one or more currencies increased as more financial market participants were attracted to European markets. The potential for destabilizing speculation inspired European Commission officials – led by Tommaso Padoa-Schioppa and Jacques Delors – to argue in favor of the replacement of the EMS with a single currency (Padoa-Schioppa 1987; Delors 1989). Their goal was to eliminate market speculation by irrevocably fixing exchange rates between participating countries.

But irrevocably fixing exchange rates in the form of a formal monetary union required even greater commitment to reduce negative externalities related to the impact of government spending on price inflation and so the negotiation of the Maastricht Treaty included convergence criteria that extended to the conduct of fiscal policy. Such commitments went beyond what market participants were willing to accept as credible and so they attacked the EMS in 1992 and 1993, pushing the United Kingdom out of the ERM and threatening the single currency as a project (Gros and Thygesen 1998: 191–234).

In response, European political leaders doubled down on the convergence requirements through the promotion of a Stability and Growth Pact, continuing the EU's shift away from a club-like arrangement (Heipertz and Verdun 2010). They also loosened the way they enforced the ERM to make it harder for market participants – often investors located outside the European Union but trading on European currency markets – to push members out. The result had different effects on different countries. The British refused to participate in an arrangement that required so much constraint on domestic macroeconomic policy as enforced by multilateral surveillance; the Italians embraced the need for external support and self-discipline (Della Sala 1998).

Other countries – like Spain, Portugal, and Greece – saw the logic behind the joint provision of monetary stability even if this implied considerable restraints on the conduct of domestic politics. The result was again to broaden participation and so set the stage for the launch of a single currency with eleven members in 1999, adding Greece as a twelfth soon after. This success led to a broadening of monetary stability but strengthened the potential for negative externalities – particularly given that the currency area included such heterogenous participants (Moses 2017). The implications became apparent the first time the Stability and Growth Pact was tested in 2003. The French and German governments refused to abide by the rules they had adopted and instead sought to reform the Stability and Growth Pact in 2005 to give themselves greater flexibility (Heipertz and Verdun 2010).

Such flexibility was not the solution to the problems of the euro area. Member states realized that the solution was greater macroeconomic policy coordination during the economic and financial crisis that started in the United States in 2007. This is when the shift to the single currency as a common-pool resource solidified. The introduction of new regulations to reinforce the Stability and Growth Pact – the "Two Pack," the "Six Pack," and the "Fiscal Compact" – bound national governments to a form of austerity that proved self-destructive (Moses 2017). The nature of the coordination problem that the Europeans faced derived from the behavior of financial market participants – many of whom were located outside Europe – who had taken advantage of the creation of the single currency to diversify their holdings of cross-border investments only to unwind those positions suddenly, reversing cross border capital flows, following the onset of the crisis (Fagan and Gaspar 2008; Merler and Pisani-Ferry 2012).

European policymakers slowly recognized this distinction between the effects of monetary integration (irrevocable fixing of exchange rates) and financial market integration (gradual development of cross-border investments followed by a sudden unwinding of accumulated positions). In response, they introduced an even greater reinforcement of the governance mechanisms and an even heavier reliance on multilateral surveillance and conditionality – which extended to include macroeconomic imbalances as well as fiscal policy. They also embarked on a new agenda to complete Europe's economic and monetary union with institutions that would underpin the efficiency of European financial integration with institutions to promote greater financial stability (Juncker et al. 2015). This is mutual coercion, mutually agreed upon. What had started as a club-good turned into a common-pool resource. As a result, the debate over an effective macroeconomic governance framework has taken on existential significance for the European project (Chang 2023).

4.3 The Single Financial Space: From Mutual Recognition to Banking Union

The evolution of European financial market integration necessarily connects the creation of the single market with the creation of the single currency. The First Banking Directive in 1977 was an attempt to bring finance into the common market; the 1987 Tommaso Padoa-Schioppa Report was an argument about the need for monetary integration to run alongside the liberalization of national capital markets (Padoa-Schioppa 1987). The liberalization of capital flows in the late 1980s was at the center of the project to match the funds available in countries with surplus savings with the investment opportunities in those countries that needed capital through the creation of a single financial space. Such cross-border capital flows would increase the efficiency of European capital markets by raising the return available to savers while lowering the cost of capital for firms looking to invest in innovation, technology, or machinery (Blanchard and Giavazzi 2002).

The problem policymakers faced is that capital market liberalization is not enough to encourage cross-border capital flows (Feldstein and Horioka 1980). To achieve that outcome, it is also necessary to create the conditions for financial firms to move funds across national boundaries in the confidence that they will be able to get that money back. Exchange rate stability is one precondition; the mutual recognition of financial firms by national authorities is another (Blanchard and Giavazzi 2002).

European financial market integration started within the single market along very light-touch principles that treated banks (as firms) like any other tradeable goods and services (Story and Walter 1997). This led to a consolidation of banking within countries and then a surge in cross-border mergers and acquisitions both inside the EU and involving firms located outside (Mügge 2010). This combination exceeded all expectations as interest rates converged across countries within the single market; that convergence then spread to non-member countries on the borders of the single market that looked likely to join the European Union (Hoffmann 2013). Here we see the influence of individuals and firms both inside and outside the European Union on the functioning of European financial markets.

As trade became easier and exchange rates became more stable in the 1990s, this convergence of interest rates continued until the differences in borrowing costs were all but eliminated. In terms of capital market efficiency, this constituted a major success. But the benefits spread far beyond the European marketplace as non-European investors expanded their positions in European markets and European investors expanded their holdings abroad (Mügge 2010).

By the start of the 2000s, European policy makers began to realize that the growth of financial institutions in Europe had begun to create problems for national regulatory oversight – particularly as countries managed to integrate with European financial markets even though they did not belong to the single market or have any prospect of joining the single currency (Mügge 2010). Europe's financial club found it difficult to exclude non-members from the benefits of membership. They also began to realize that financial stability no longer focused only on individual institutions – micro-prudential risk – but also took on systemic properties as large financial institutions became dependent upon one another both inside and outside Europe.

This was not a new realization. The globalization of finance started already in the 1970s – around the time of the First Banking Directive – and financial market regulations began coordinating across countries then as well (Story and Walter 1997). Nevertheless, the level of concern and the need for tighter coordination was much greater than in the past. Therefore, policymakers looked for ways to promote industry self-regulation – relying on what came to be known as the Lamfalussy process (Lamfalussy 2001). Figure 11 maps this evolution in governance arrangements. As in the other two case studies, the focus is on the European response to the actions of firms and individuals, rather than highlighting the behavior of those non-state actors directly.

European efforts to gain greater control over financial institutions and financial markets shifted the EU away from a club-like arrangement toward a regime involving greater self-restraint and multilateral surveillance like we would expect to find in the administration of common-pool resources. At the same time, however, the emphasis in the Lamfalussy process on self-regulation within the financial industry strengthened the competitive position of the largest cross-border banks while weakening the oversight of national regulatory authorities (Posner 2007). This was true particularly in Central and Eastern Europe, where large West European banks assumed an outsized role in providing financial services (Epstein 2017).

The global economic and financial crisis that began in 2007 revealed the weakness of European financial market regulation. It also triggered a sudden reversal of many years of cross-border investments. This reversal is what created turbulence in sovereign debt markets as a major negative externality (Merler and Pisani-Ferry 2012). The policy response was to promote a more centralized form of financial market regulation through the creation of European financial regulatory authorities (De Larosière 2009). It was also to negotiate with West European banks to ensure that they would not abandon Central and East European markets (Epstein 2017). This combination of factors

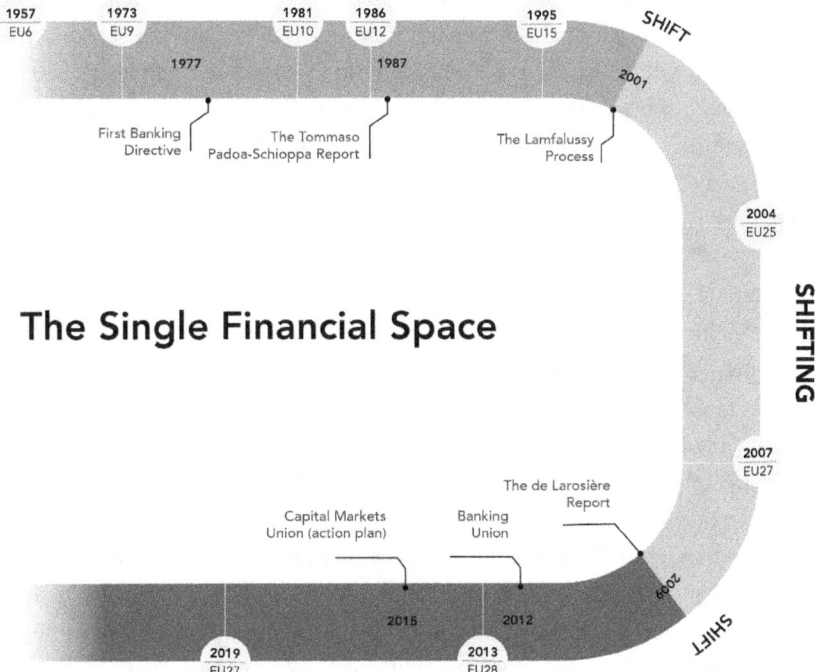

Figure 11 The Europeanization of finance

Note: The figure highlights three phases in the evolution of the good. The outer edge marks the years of enlargement and the membership count. The inner edge features the main documents or decisions that confirm the governance arrangements specific to the nature of the good in that period.

completed the shift of the single financial space away from being a club good to becoming something much closer to a common-pool resource.

Nevertheless, that response proved inadequate to stabilize either the banks or sovereign debt markets. Sovereign debt markets in Spain and Italy looked likely to collapse, implicating their financial systems as well as their public finances (Van Rompuy 2014). Worse, the collapse of those countries could not be contained within their national boundaries. Both the single European financial space and the single currency were at risk. The only solution was for the ECB to step in as lender of last resort. To do so, however, the ECB required the creation of a much stronger single supervisory mechanism to oversee systemically significant financial institutions and a common rulebook for financial oversight. Powerful member states, like Germany, insisted on such provisions as well. European policymakers also agreed to the creation of a permanent bailout authority in the form of the European Stability Mechanism and promised to move toward a fully articulated "banking union" (Howarth and Quaglia 2016). While these reforms were designed to enhance the efficiency and stability of European financial markets, they were hailed as an effort to complete Europe's economic and monetary union (Juncker et al. 2015).

That linkage between the single currency and the single financial space was not simply rhetorical. The two goods are closely interrelated both in Europe and elsewhere (Underhill and Jones 2023). They also connect closely to the single market. Within this context, tracing the shift of the single financial space from a club-good to a common-pool resource shows that the stability of the European project hinges critically on its ability to manage the negative externalities associated with the behavior of its many financial market participants – meaning both state actors and non-state actors alike. In turn, these actors require much more intrusive governance arrangements that entail greater self-discipline and more extensive multilateral surveillance. Enlargement is part of this process, sometimes as a solution to the need for greater control over firms and individuals who compete for access and sometimes as a stimulus for further integration. Mutual coercion, mutually agreed upon works at many levels in this context; deepening and widening are closely interconnected.

4.4 Connecting Common-Pool Resources

The European single market, single currency, and single financial space no longer operate as club goods with light-touch governance arrangements to ensure each member state enjoys net benefits. Instead, the governance arrangements focus on procedures to protect the rule of law, ensure the effective coordination of macroeconomic policies, and underpin (and enforce) financial stability. Those procedures have developed in response to the progressively greater heterogeneity of member states. They focus on the prevention of free riding. And they also suffer from problems associated with congestion in terms of decision making. That is why the enforcement provisions of the new framework for protection of the rule of law are found wanting (Södersten 2023), the framework for macroeconomic policy coordination remains controversial (Buti and Fabbrini 2023), and the banking union remains incomplete (Pierret and Howarth 2023).

In economic terms, the EU is no longer a club, but something that looks more like an administrator of common-pool resources. And those common-pool resources are interconnected. That was the most important lesson provided by the global economic and financial crisis: A failure to maintain financial stability can undermine the functioning of the internal market and even jeopardize the survival of the single currency. It was the lesson of the pandemic: The need to shut down the movement of people to stop the spread of contagion risks bringing down the banks, fracturing the single currency. And that lesson was the central insight ECB President Mario Draghi had when he promised to do "whatever it takes" to safeguard the euro: A collapse of the single currency – what Draghi called convertibility risk – would disrupt the single market and undermine financial stability. As a self-governing collective of common-pool resources, the EU provides essential goods. The challenge for the European Union is to ensure that the way those goods are accessed does not lead to their exhaustion.

5 The European Union as a Security Provider

Whatever has an impact on European economic integration, necessarily also has implications for European security. This has always been the case. The European Union has fostered peace and security among its members since the start of the European project in the aftermath of the Second World War. In that sense, the EU has never only been a civilian power, but also a security community. Importantly, the EU was not Europe's only security provider. The North Atlantic Treaty Organization played an important role in holding off the external threat posed by the Soviet Union (Sloan 2003). But the European project was a critical source of internal stability, fostering the reconciliation of former enemies, encouraging the growth in prosperity and interdependence, supporting the effective use of multilateral institutions, and promoting the protection of human rights (McCormick 2007).

As suggested in the introduction, the security provided by the European Union has many of the classic traits of a public good, particularly when understood mostly in terms of "defense" (Foldvary 1994: 8; Rothschild 1995). In the case of Europe, it could be easily claimed that the protection received by any one European or EU member state should not subtract from the protection extended to any other. As Charles Kindleberger (1986: 2) pointed out in his Presidential Address to the American Economic Association, the identification of security (or, better, defense) as a public good in terms of economic theory goes back to Adam Smith.

Some scholars, however, have argued that security is at best an imperfect public good. The reason, they argue, is that the resources used to provide security do not necessary serve the same function in different contexts, they cannot be deployed at the same time against all (or all types of) threats, and their use implies both a distribution of resources and benefits that may not overlap. In such a context, we should expect to see conflicts over both membership and burden-sharing in any security community – leading to optimal sizing considerations that are more reminiscent of clubs than regimes governing public goods (Sandler 1977).

Scholars continued to observe and explain this tension between the status of security as an "impure" public good and a club good well after the EU also increased its membership. Some noticed security could only be seen as a public good if "defined as the absence of threat," but it is a club good "if defined in terms of deterrence" (Krahmann 2008: 386). We suggest that this tension can be resolved once we accept the dynamic nature of security, and its broader meaning beyond a hard military focus. In this section we show that European security began with a high level of excludability and low rivalry, being much closer to a club good than a public good, and it evolved to lower excludability and high rivalry, characteristic of a common-pool resource. As with the other goods we analyzed previously, this change ran in parallel with an increasing intrusiveness of European governance arrangements. Sauli Niinistö (2024: 5, 10) referred to this transformation in terms of "strategic responsibility":

> A common interest like preparedness requires common responsibility. Each individual has a stake in building and maintaining security, for example by choosing what kind of information sources we trust. Understanding everyone's responsibility for their own security and that of those closest to them makes it easier to accept the actions and investment needed from Member States and the EU to build stronger preparedness.

Tracing the evolution of the EU as a security provider, we show that security is not only subject to rivalry in consumption and optimal size considerations (Sandler 1977), but also prone to both under-provision and overuse. Within that context, we show that there are analytical gains to be had from charting the evolution of European security from a club good, albeit impure, to a common-pool resource, just as in the case of other goods the EU generates and administers. By implication, there are key moments in the development of the European Union as an organization that led to an increasing reliance for the provision of collective security on the kind of governance arrangements that are characteristic of the management of common-pool resources. The difference in this case compared to the economic cases analyzed earlier is that the European response is not only – or even primarily – to the behavior of non-state actors. As Niinistö (2024) underscores, security and defense are areas where nation states and the European Union have significant agency. Nevertheless, the pattern of response is similar: EU enlargement and institutional reform were influenced by the same

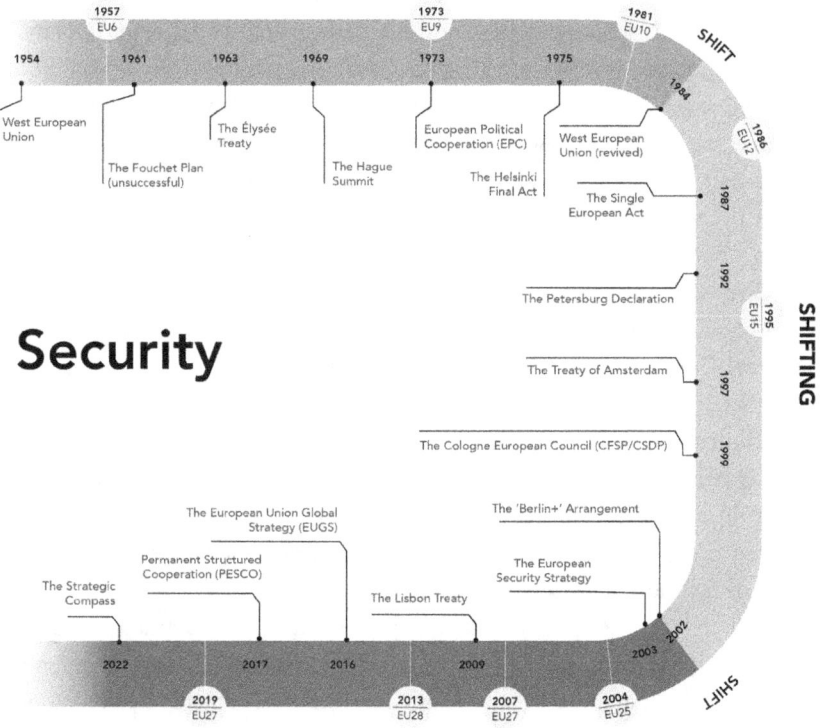

Figure 12 Europe's progressive embrace of security

Note: The figure highlights three phases in the evolution of the good. The outer edge marks the years of enlargement and the membership count. The inner edge features the main documents or decisions that confirm the governance arrangements specific to the nature of the good in that period.

external factors even as the two processes – enlargement and institutional reform – also influence each other. Figure 12 maps that historical development.

5.1 Beyond German Rearmament

In the immediate aftermath of the Second World War, Germany was the Europeans' main security concern. The first postwar security arrangement, the 1948 Brussels Treaty Organization (BTO), was created by the United Kingdom, France, and the Benelux countries to counter the threat of German aggression (Willis 1968). Soon, however, a divided Germany was no longer perceived as the principal adversary. Other Europeans still worried about Germany's potential for military aggression, but the Soviet Union quickly emerged as the main threat to European security. The Europeans convinced the United States to form NATO and include the original BTO members, adding Canada, Denmark, Italy, Norway, and Portugal into the new arrangement.

The price for the United States to participate in NATO was to bring together the three zones of occupied Germany administered by Britain, France, and the United States with an eye to integrate this Western part of Germany into the European economy (Sloan 2003; Segers 2023). The challenge for the Europeans was to come up with a plan that would not result in a remilitarization of Germany. The Schuman Declaration presented by French foreign minister Robert Schuman on May 9, 1950 proposed the creation of a European Coal and Steel Community (ECSC) with peacebuilding in mind. According to the logic that led to the creation of the ECSC, pooling together coal and steel production would establish a sort of solidarity that "will make it plain that any war between France and Germany becomes not merely unthinkable, but materially impossible." The security arrangement that came from the ECSC followed a tight governance arrangement that imagined deterrence through a form of mutually assured destruction.

The founding members of the ECSC, France, West Germany, Italy, the Netherlands, Belgium, and Luxembourg created security through interdependence. Countries that did not want to join the ECSC – like the United Kingdom – provided alternative security guarantees. The UK remained tied to all but Germany both through NATO and through its BTO membership. The two different kinds of commitment had starkly different implications. The UK remained an important alliance partner. By contrast, the ECSC members went beyond a formal commitment to collective security to foster a "security community" in which ever more intensive economic interaction would help foster a sense of solidarity if not common identity (Deutsch et al. 1957). When those original ECSC members added the common market to their portfolio of "communities," they reinforced the appearance of this new European construct as a "club" for wealthy West European countries, but they also reinforced Europe's evolution into the kind of security community that Niinistö (2024) sketches in his report on European resilience and security, with governance arrangements better suited to the administration of common-pool resources.

To show this evolution from club to common-pool resource, we start the security analysis with the acceptance of West German rearmament to counter the Soviet threat and the conversion of the Brussels Treaty Organization into the West European Union (WEU) in 1954. That conversion also changed the fourth preamble of the Brussels treaty from guaranteeing that members would "take such steps as may be held to be necessary in the event of a renewal by Germany of a policy of aggression" to "promote the unity and to encourage the progressive integration of Europe." And the WEU added Italy and West Germany as members alongside the original five, which included Britain. Our analysis focuses on that goal of progressive integration.

The attempts to build a European security arrangement combined a strategy of internalization and externalization (Howorth 2012). When Europeans created the European Economic Community (1957), they externalized security matters to NATO under U.S. leadership (Sloan 2003). In that sense, the EEC formally started as a civilian power. But an internalized version of European defense was provided through the WEU. The member governments defined the limits of their security community as an exclusive club with common goals – coordinating to deter Soviet threats. While formally a civilian power, the EU emerged as a security community in practice through its overlap with the WEU.

5.2 The EU as a Security Club

Accepting that member states will maintain full sovereignty of their foreign affairs made it easier to build the new Europe as a club. Indeed, when French President Charles De Gaulle tried to introduce security considerations into the EEC via the Fouchet Plan, the Dutch government pushed hard to retain a more focused mission. In return, De Gaulle vetoed the first British application to join the EEC at least in part because it conflicted with his vision for a European security community (Silj 1967). Instead, De Gaulle focused on the Franco–German relationship and, through the Elysée Treaty (1963), sought to build a parallel arrangement with a more explicit foreign policy and security dimension. While the Elysée Treaty formalized the end of centuries of Franco–German enmity, it did not immediately foster greater European integration in matters of security. If anything, it deepened divisions between the WEU and the European Community while at the same time driving a wedge between De Gaulle and more Atlanticist voices in Germany and the Netherlands.

The challenge to maintain this security arrangement came with the combination of war in Vietnam, Prague Spring, and détente. The replacement of Charles de Gaulle by Georges Pompidou gave a new impetus to EEC relations with the United Kingdom. At the Hague Summit of 1969, a committee of the political directors of the six EEC foreign ministries accepted the task to design proposals on foreign policy issues toward closer political integration at the European level. By 1973, to respond more effectively to the rising tensions between the United States and the Soviet Union, European countries decided to coordinate with one another via the process of European Political Cooperation. Accepting to enlarge to include British participation would add weight to the

European voice in global affairs. Hence, it became harder for the European Community to reject the British application and easier to embrace the idea of British membership. When opening to the British, the EEC also opened to other countries from the European Free Trade Association – namely, Denmark, Ireland, and Norway. And while the Norwegians ultimately chose not to join, the Danish and the Irish did, bringing significant diversity in terms of their understanding of both security and economic relationships. Heterogeneity increased and excludability decreased. Governance arrangements, however, were still to adapt to the new conditions.

The accession of the United Kingdom (plus Denmark and Ireland) came at a cost in terms of the internal cohesion of the EEC, but it delivered a benefit in terms of European coordination within NATO and the transatlantic relationship. The extent of the transformative effect of UK accession for the EEC should not be exaggerated. That coordination across the Atlantic did not address security concerns directly. Outside NATO, Europeans tried to work together to address major challenges in global politics through the development of international summitry, focusing more clearly on economic exchanges and a new human rights dimension (Thomas 2001). That European understanding of the source of security in multilateralism was manifested in the Helsinki Final Act.

Signed in 1975 by all European states (except Albania), the Soviet Union, the United States and Canada, the Helsinki Final Act was meant to lower the tensions of the Cold War through multilateral engagement. Nevertheless, when the Soviet Union deployed SS-20 intermediate range ballistic missiles on its European territories and close enough to reach Western Europe a year later, the West European model of loose security arrangements left its members at a disadvantage. The EU's inability to keep managing security as a club good became evident.

5.3 Mapping the Shift

In the context of an increased threat from the Soviet Union, uncertainty about U.S. military commitment, and increased heterogeneity among the members of the European Community, a shift from club to a system of common-pool resources started taking place toward the end of the 1970s and the beginning of the 1980s. It is during this period that we start to observe a further tightening of governance arrangements to respond to evolving security pressures.

When the Cold War intensified after the Soviet invasion of Afghanistan in 1979 and with the election of Ronald Reagan in 1980, the reaction of the French and German governments was to strengthen their bilateral security cooperation and to relaunch the WEU. The French and Germans even agreed to the creation of a joint brigade to be based inside Germany. That "Europeanization" of security was necessary to help the German government implement the "double-track" decision for responding to the threat of Soviet intermediate range ballistic weapons (SS-20s) by allowing the United States to station nuclear weapons on German soil. This time, however, the goal was not to construct a parallel arrangement, but rather to consolidate this explicitly European security identity as a first step to absorbing the WEU within the European Community.

European governments felt they had no voice in the conversation between superpowers and worried their interests would be ignored. This was true both when U.S. President Ronald Reagan heightened tensions with the Soviet Union in the early 1980s and when Reagan embraced détente and an aggressive approach to nuclear arms control later that same decade (Gavin 2015). To strengthen their position between the United States and the Soviet Union, Europeans continued to tighten the security arrangements between themselves. At this point, the heterogeneity of EEC members had increased with the enlargements of 1981 and 1986. Altogether, Greece, Spain, and Portugal had different security interests in bolstering their own domestic stability or, in the case of Greece, for its protection against potential Turkish aggression.

Europeans used the Single European Act (1987) to institutionalize European Political Cooperation and so lay the foundations for what would become CFSP. The idea was not to promote the European Community as a rival to NATO, but rather to take advantage of the European Community as a governance arrangement to attempt to coordinate different European positions within the NATO alliance and vis-à-vis the United States and the Soviet Union. The type of security Europeans envisaged for themselves did not mean independent military force projection; it meant strengthening their role in how NATO's politico-military strategies would look like. The challenge was to strengthen a common European identity or voice.

The end of the Cold War created the opportunity for the European Community to develop a distinctive European security identity and the unification of Germany provided the stimulus for the transformation of the European Community into a European Union. The shift away from the club-good features of European security continued as security as a good become even more rivalrous among members with different risk perceptions. Although it could be argued that such rivalry matters more for NATO than for the European Union, insofar as NATO has greater control over physical military resources and greater responsibility to push back against physical security threats, the European Council has other constraints. It has only limited time to debate security challenges and it can present a common policy only when there is prior agreement. Moreover, the

European Council sought to get more involved in the physical security business, where resource rivalry would become more prominent.

Security for the Europeans continued to mean something different from the military force projection that defined an organization like NATO. In 1992, the ministers of the Western European Union adopted the Petersburg Declaration to define the organization's military tasks of a humanitarian, peacekeeping and peacemaking nature. The 1993 Maastricht Treaty also set the objective to build up the WEU in stages as the defense component of the European Union. This direction made it more attractive both for formally neutral countries like Sweden, Finland, and Austria to join the European Union but also for the European Union to embrace those countries for membership. Nevertheless, this new vocation placed clear demands on European resources in terms of personnel, equipment, finances, and time for deliberation.

This soft European security identity revealed important differences in the security interests of the member states. As a result, it was not immediately effective. The different member states disagreed on how to coordinate their foreign policy and how to promote their common interests. Member State heterogeneity and rivalry over priorities became increasingly more visible. This could be seen most clearly in the debates around the violent breakup of Yugoslavia and in the relative ineffectiveness of European efforts to manage those conflicts. It could also be seen in the European Union's establishment of formal criteria for membership in the 1993 Copenhagen Summit that would be hard to meet (Anghel and Jones 2022).

With the signing of the Amsterdam Treaty in 1997, member states agreed to enact a CFSP. This slowly moved the conversation on the EU's role in dealing with its own security interests (Hofmann 2013). It also ensured that the Petersberg tasks performed by the WEU would be taken over by the European Union. The violence surrounding the dissolution of Yugoslavia and U.S. insistence that Europeans take over some of the financial burdens of NATO led the United Kingdom to drop its opposition to the introduction of European autonomous defense capacities. As a result, UK Prime Minister Tony Blair and French President Jacques Chirac signed the 1998 Saint-Malo declaration that advanced the creation of a European Security and Defense Policy.

Nevertheless, the de facto establishment of coordinated autonomous defense capacities for the EU remained an incomplete process. This third condition of tighter governance arrangements was still not met, but increased rivalry among members and lower exclusivity were already evident. Again, the problem lay in the fact that the EU can only pursue a common foreign and security policy when the member states have common agreement. The EU also depends on resources provided on an ad hoc basis by individual member states. Member states lacking adequate resources to pursue their priorities independently had to wait until other member states were willing and capable to make up the gap.

The need for stronger coordination became increasingly apparent in the late 1990s. In June 1999, the Cologne European Council decided to absorb the WEU into the European Union. That decision led to the creation of a European Security and Defence Policy (ESDP). Through this instrument, Europeans pursued the political integration of Europe and the formation of a European identity to support a common foreign policy with no particular enemy in mind (Merand 2008: 3). The 1999 Cologne Council took place as the wars in former Yugoslavia culminated in NATO's bombing of Serbia and Kosovo. At this Council, the EU also appointed the last WEU Secretary General, Javier Solana, as the High Representative for Common Foreign and Security Policy as a further move to centralize and tighten governance arrangements over the provision of security.

In the absence of a robust EU security agenda, however, the NATO bombing of Kosovo and Serbia created a sense in the European Council and the European Commission that the enlargement process could be a second-best option to generate peace in Europe. Enlargement to postcommunist countries thus became a security imperative. The result was a much broader and faster expansion of the European Union than had been initially intended in the early 1990s (Anghel and Jones 2022).

The EU also moved to strengthen its relative autonomy. It forged an agreement with NATO to access NATO assets for use in security operations not involving the United States, and it drew up a first European Security Strategy. This activity took place before the European Union expanded to Central and Eastern Europe in 2004, but in the clear knowledge that enlargement would happen and that the member states of the European Union – both old and new, and among the original fifteen member states – were deeply divided over the George W. Bush administration's determination to invade Iraq. The EU was no longer a security club of relatively like-minded members, it was increasingly divided, conflictive, and ineffective at asserting its identity.

5.4 Security as a Common-Pool Resource

As with other common-pool resources that the EU administers, the requirements for tighter governance structures to manage security increased significantly. The Treaty of Lisbon (2009) formalized cooperation between the EU and NATO, increasing the actorness of the EU in international security. Moreover, at the behest of countries who wanted a stronger role for the EU on defense, the mutual defense clause inscribed in Article 4 of the Paris Treaty that had established the West European Union was kept in Article 42.7 of the Treaty of the European Union, as amended by the Treaty of Lisbon. According to this article "If a Member State is the victim of armed aggression on its territory, the other Member States shall have towards it an obligation of aid and assistance by all the means in their power, in accordance with Article 51 of the United Nations Charter." Governing security through a mutual defense clause moved ownership of security onto all members.

The pressure to extend security provisions to more countries slowed during the first decade of the twenty-first Century and all but ground to a halt during the second. And this time, countries like Ukraine and Georgia experienced democratic revolutions in the early 2000s (Popova and Shevel 2023), while Russia started to reveal the failure of its democratic transition (Snegovaya 2023). But the European Union felt little imperative to embrace these threatened countries as candidates for membership or to recognize Russia as a security threat. Instead, the European Commission developed a "neighborhood policy" and an Eastern partnership with the idea that these countries would remain close and yet outside. Countries outside the EU grew to depend on perceived EU force projection to deter Russia aggression. While the credibility of some EU political or economic sanctions existed, the EU's neighborhood benefitted from a (fragile) security umbrella.

The sense of security threats coming from the countries of the Western Balkans also weakened over time. Although the EU played an active role in the stabilization of the region, those countries made little progress in their efforts to "Europeanize" and start the accession process, let alone complete it (Džankić, Keil and Kmezić 2018). Only Croatia eventually qualified for membership. The EU recognized security threats emanating from the Balkans as part of its internal costs and attempted to mitigate them through structural support. However, this approach proved ineffective, as the EU's capacity to maintain clear firewalls between itself and its southeastern neighbors gradually eroded.

Moreover, the EU remained reluctant to recognize Russia as a security threat and integrate the costs of that security threat in its plans to protect European security. Instead, the EU continued to extend the same logic of intertwining economies to improve peaceful coexistence in its policy toward Russia. Since the EU and Russia signed a Partnership and Cooperation Agreement on December 1, 1997, the two actors held a total of thirty-two summits. According to the speech of the High Representative Catherine Ashton on the eve of the EU-Russia Summit of December 13, 2011, the EU was a first mover in including Russia in the World Trade Organization: "As Russia's largest trading partner by far, the EU is a crucial partner in the 18-years long negotiations." Ashton continues by adding that "As we remove barriers to trade, travel and exchange, the outlook and expectations of our citizens can be expected more and more to converge and the fundamental interest in co-operation will increase."[14] Such summits continued even after Russia's invasion of Georgia in 2008.

Rivalry over how to build security also increased inside the EU system. This notion of rivalry is different from one based on the allocation of scarce resources and focuses on the conflicts that emerge across different conceptions of security – like energy security and physical security. While the German government saw increasing investment in natural gas pipelines with Russia as a source of energy security, the Polish government saw the same investments as increasing the threat of Russian aggression that might destabilize Poland's border with Ukraine. Such conflicts are frequent in the management of common-pool resources. Water can be used for drinking, cooling, recreation, irrigation, and waste disposal. Forests can be used for shade, fuel, building, and the protection of biodiversity. Finding a way to reconcile competing demands on natural resources is similar to the reconciliation of different demands for security in that respect.

Such conflicts were not limited to Germany and Poland. The disaggregated character of the European Union's Common Foreign and Security Policy gave member states considerable flexibility to devise their own approach to bilateral relations (Davis Cross and Karolewski 2017). This permitted Russia to build relations of trust with favorable European politicians and parties, creating its own "Trojan Horses" within the EU (Orenstein and Kelemen 2017). Those relationships proved beneficial to Russia's anti-Western interests in the long run and diminished European security. As a result, the evolution of security as a common-pool resource required increased coordination to prevent the depletion of the security-good among European countries with rivalrous interests (Anghel 2020). But the lack of enthusiasm for building a coherent CFSP remained the norm. Europeans failed to coordinate on the requirements for effective deterrence.

The European Union's long-standing dependence on Russia for energy, particularly natural gas, played a crucial role in the way member states defined their security goals. That dependence determined the will and pace with which Europeans could recast their foreign and economic policies toward Russia once Vladimir Putin's authoritarian and anti-Western stances became more apparent around 2011–2012. The EU decreased its energy, economic, cyber, and military security when trying to balance between pursuing cooperation with Russia and maintaining a common security goal even after Russia's annexation of Crimea in 2014.

---

[14] www.consilium.europa.eu/uedocs/cms_Data/docs/pressdata/EN/foraff/126907.pdf

Eastern members, unlike their Western counterparts, were rattled to the core by Russia's aggressive actions and tried to persuade the United States of the need to invest more in NATO's Eastern Flank. They did not pursue a united European front but confirmed the bloc's heterogeneity. The EU's Eastern Flank signed a joint declaration in 2015 aimed at redirecting more of NATO's attention to the region.[15] Yet, the debates among EU member states that followed showed regional rifts as southern European EU members systematically prioritized threats emanating from the Middle East and North Africa, while those in the east pointed to Russia.

In the years between Russia's annexation of Crimea in 2014 and its full-scale invasion of Ukraine in 2022, the United States and its European allies argued over the construction of gas pipelines with Russia and the risks associated with increasing European dependence on Russian energy resources (Demarais 2022). Those arguments did not end in a joint European commitment to find way to shake off European dependence on Russian gas and maintain economic growth. During the decade prior to the full-scale invasion of Ukraine in 2022, the European Union's dependence on Russian natural gas continued to increase, reaching 41.1 percent of gross available energy derived from natural gas in 2020.[16] A significant portion of the EU's natural gas imports came from pipelines like Nord Stream and TurkStream facilitating the transportation of gas to European markets. Russia's top pipeline gas consumer in the EU was also its largest economy, Germany.

Germany's excessive energy dependence on Russia limited the ability of the EU to challenge Russian President Vladimir Putin's growing authoritarianism by targeting its energy sector through sanctions (Dyson 2016). Built on the legacy of a cooperative approach in its foreign policy vis-à-vis Moscow since 1969 – known as *Ostpolitik* – Germany's interlocking of its economic development with the import of Russian gas made it particularly predisposed to cooperation with Russia (Siddi 2016). Germany's reluctance to shake off its dependence on Russian gas and the start of the construction of Nord Stream 2 in 2016 increased threats to European security. Even so, German Chancellor Angela Merkel remained committed to the Nord Stream 2 project which was completed in 2021.

---

[15] See the Joint Declaration on "Allied Solidarity and Shared Responsibility," (November 4, 2015). www.atlanticcouncil.org/blogs/natosource/nine-heads-of-state-call-on-alliance-to-strengthen-the-eastern-flank-of-nato/.

[16] The data can be found here 'EU energy mix and import dependency', *Eurostat: Statistics Explained* (Brussels: European Commission, March 2022) https://ec.europa.eu/eurostat/statistics-explained/index.php?title=Archive:EU_energy_mix_and_import_dependency#EU_energy_dependency_on_Russia

Furthermore, the EU's ability to enforce a unified approach toward Russia has been hindered by the divergent foreign policies pursued by certain member states, often influenced by leaders such as Viktor Orbán in Hungary, Robert Fico in Slovakia, and political parties like the Lega in Italy, the National Front in France, the Alternative for Germany, the Austrian Freedom Party, and the Austrian People's Party. These actors, through their pro-Putin stances and policies, challenge the EU's efforts to present a unified front on matters concerning Russia's geopolitical ambitions and security threats to today.

To counter such internal rivalries, the EU articulated a European Union Global Strategy in 2016 and developed the Permanent Structured Cooperation in 2017. The Strategic Compass, agreed on in 2022 was meant to strengthen the EU's fledgling CFSP in ways that would discourage individual members from pursuing contradictory international agendas.

5.5 Connecting Security to Economics

Russia's full-scale invasion of Ukraine in 2022 confronted the EU with the weakness of its military defense. More important, it revealed the extent to which European security and European economic performance were connected via European dependence on energy ties with Russia, manufacturing ties with China, critical raw materials and agricultural ties with Ukraine, population flows with Africa and the Middle East, and financial, technological, and energy links with the United States. Russia's full-scale invasion of Ukraine disrupted the functioning of the internal market by jeopardizing access to energy resources and critical raw materials, by cutting off and then rerouting the flow of agricultural products from Ukraine, by displacing millions of Ukrainian citizens, and through the imposition of sanctions and counter sanctions. The collapse of Ukraine in the face of Russian aggression would only make matters worse – as would any expansion of the conflict to Moldova or Georgia.

Meanwhile, Russian and Chinese involvement in the Western Balkans creates other challenges. The experience of North Macedonia is not just a cautionary tale. It is an ongoing problem across the Western Balkans that the EU can most easily address through the leverage provided by accession negotiations and eventual EU membership. To protect Europe's single market, single currency, and single financial space, the EU needed an economic security strategy as well as a military one. That is why the European Council asked Enrico Letta to write on the single market and the European Commission asked Mario Draghi to write on competitiveness and Sauli Niinistö to write on resilience all in the same year. These reports necessarily speak to one another through the language of security as well as prosperity.

The European Union also needed to consolidate its frontiers both to ensure their political stability and to protect against the threat that other countries would use EU neighbours as staging points for efforts to undermine European economic security. The result was the revival of enlargement as a tool for the generation of security. In the aftermath of Russia's full-scale invasion of 2022, the European Union extended candidate status to Ukraine, Moldova and Georgia. The EU also worked to accelerate the accession process across the Western Balkans. Nothing has changed within these countries to make them more attractive for membership from an economic perspective and few observers imagine they will easily qualify according to the criteria set in Copenhagen. Nevertheless, the pressure continues to mount to bring Ukraine and Moldova into the European Union as a way for the EU to better control its defense capabilities.

The difficulty for the EU in denying a membership prospect to Ukraine, Moldova, Georgia, and the countries of the Western Balkans becomes more visible when we juxtapose the European Union's general reluctance to expand its formal membership because of the implications for institutional reform, with the need to bring Ukraine as close as possible and as fast as possible to make the perspective of membership credible. In this way, the evolution of the European Union as a security community reinforced the transformation of this organization by reducing the exclusivity of the arrangement and increasing the heterogeneity of the membership. As with other goods that the EU generates and administers, this shift changed the nature of security from a club good to a common-pool resource.

6 Conclusion

The focus for this "Element" is on the logic behind how the European Union has developed both in terms of the way the organization works and the way it has expanded to include new member states. That logic derives from the study of clubs and common-pool resources. Our argument is that the European Union may have started as a club, where members agreed to light-touch arrangements to generate and govern non-rivalrous goods from which only they could benefit, but it quickly evolved into something more closely resembling a system of common-pool resources, where members have to manage attractive goods in a competitive or rivalrous context. The governance arrangements had to deepen and widen in ways that imposed greater obligations on increasing numbers of governments to avoid the depletion of the goods EU member states depend on.

In making this claim, we accept the critique of those who argue that the reasons for EU enlargement extend beyond economic rationality (Schimmelfennig and Sedelmeier 2002). Nevertheless, we argue, the economic theory of goods from which the notion of club goods is derived has enduring merit in helping us to understand how European enlargement interacts with the more general process of European integration. Our proposal is to complement the club-goods approach that has gained significant traction in the literature by drawing upon a different branch of the economic theory of goods and to regard the EU as a system of common-pool resources. We believe this pivot is warranted insofar as the governance of common-pool resources deals explicitly with the challenges faced in sustaining the production of low exclusivity and high rivalry goods.

While our theorizing is inspired by contemporary EU decisions related to the revival of enlargement, our argument presents a different model of European governance arrangements beyond the decision to admit new member states. In this model, the enlargement process should be seen as a set of rules, among others, that the EU deploys to control the potential for the overconsumption of its resources and an institutional opportunity to limit some of the ensuing rivalry among its members and tightly connected non-members.

We argued that thinking about the European Union as a club that administers exclusive and non-rivalrous goods sheds important light on how the organization works and yet fails to explain what happens when the goods the EU provides become more easily accessible to non-members, when membership increases, and when the consumption of the goods by any one member begins to compete with the access to that good (or the successful production of the good) for all the rest. In effect, and over time, the EU becomes less exclusive and the consumption of the goods it provides becomes more rivalrous. In this way, the organization evolves from being a club to something that more closely resembles a system that administers common-pool resources, with important implications in terms of its governance.

The internal logic of the EU as responsible for the administration of overlapping common-pool resources is consistent with the European Council's decision to reform in response to an external shock and to extend a membership prospect to Ukraine, Moldova, Georgia, and the Western Balkans. Moreover, that logic cuts across the traditional deepening-versus-widening debate, just as it cuts across the usual debates about whether institutional reform should precede or follow enlargement.

We illustrate this argument by discussing the evolution of four goods that the European Union generates and manages: the single market, the single currency, the single financial space, and security. We show that these no longer operate as club goods with light-touch governance arrangements to ensure each member state enjoys net benefits. Instead, the governance arrangements focus on procedures to protect the rule of law, ensure the effective coordination of macroeconomic policies, underpin (and enforce) financial stability, ensure the credibility of security commitments, and guarantee force projection. Those procedures have developed in response to different sources of pressure arising from problems associated with congestion, diversity, and freeriding from those who have access.

Elinor Ostrom's theory of common-pool resources serves to understand how management challenges call for certain solutions. We suggest that the main elements of the logic she advanced for small-scale communities can also be applied to large scale institutional designs, such as the European Union. Tracking the EU's shift from a club to something that looks more like a system of common-pool resources helps us to understand why existing member states exercise greater tolerance of diversity, shift from direct to diffuse reciprocity, accept slower and more cumbersome decision making, exercise greater self-discipline, accept more constant multilateral surveillance, focus on building trans-national solidarity and a sense of European identity, and diminish their national sovereignty. This is the essence of the kind of mutual coercion, mutually agreed upon necessary to prevent a tragedy of the commons. It also helps us to understand why that change in the nature of membership might be difficult to manage both for individual countries and for the European Union. That is why the enforcement provisions of the new framework for protection of the rule of law are found wanting (Södersten 2023), the framework for macroeconomic policy coordination remains controversial (Buti and Fabbrini 2023), the banking union remains incomplete (Pierret and Howarth 2023), and the EU remains dependent on the United States for its security (Anghel and Jones 2024).

Meanwhile, the pressure for further enlargement continues to increase to include non-members who are already benefiting from access to multiple attractive EU goods, but who have no formal role or vested interest in preserving those goods. Hence, the European Union has embarked on a new and ambitious project of enlargement to countries in Eastern Europe and in the Western Balkans (European Council 2022). Those countries will add to heterogeneity, congestion, and the risk of freeriding in one or more key areas related to the protection of the rule of law, the maintenance of sound macroeconomic policies, and the preservation of financial stability (Anghel and Dzankic 2023). The EU's investment in the transformation of candidate countries will have to be significant to ensure they play a productive role.

The heterogeneity that candidate states could bring into the governing structure of the EU is remarkable. Yet the EU has been here before. And the EU has the collective knowledge and capacities to manage the risks connected to increased heterogeneity, congestion, or freeriding. Indeed, once we correctly identify the inner logic that underpins the governance structures of the EU, we can see that enlargement is part of the EU's toolbox to deal with a complex set of interactions. Put another way, formal enlargement of the European Union to bring in new member states is just one more way of structuring public sector engagement to address the challenges raised by the increasingly attractive and less exclusive goods that the EU produces. Formal enlargement of the EU to these states as full members is not obligatory. At a certain point, however, it may be more effective to construct a more encompassing form of engagement and avoid ad-hoc solutions for each transnational interaction.

The implications of this argument are significant. Modeling the EU as an administrator of overlapping common-pool resources makes it easy to see why the European Union will need to accompany that decision to enlarge with internal reforms to strengthen self-discipline and multilateral surveillance among the member states, ultimately asking members states to transfer even more of their sovereignty to the EU. This is true particularly in the context of rule-of-law and defense policy, but it also applies for macroeconomic policy coordination and financial market integration. As the history of European integration reveals, these are all areas where the focus of attention has shifted over time from the advantages of access to the club for individual members to the challenges associated with managing the many potential negative externalities that can emerge from having increasing access to European economic goods from increasingly diverse participants whose actions can impose significant costs on each other and on the European polity as a whole.

But the EU is not alone in this sense. A similar argument applies to any international organization that expands beyond its optimal size, including security organizations (Anghel and Jones 2025). The current NATO enlargement debate reflects this, as NATO considers the costs and benefits of including countries like Ukraine, Moldova, and Georgia, which are under threat from Russia. The threat Russia and other hostile third countries pose in Europe is more than just military. To be sure, governments in many EU member states that border on Russia, Ukraine, and the Baltic Sea express concern that Russian aggression will not stop if Ukraine falls. But the consequences of a Russian victory would also be important in terms of the disruption this would pose for European supply chains, energy, and agricultural markets, for the impact it would have on population movements, for the price inflation it would create, and for the financial speculation and instability it would encourage. Similar concerns arise from the prospect that other third countries, like China, will use instability on the frontiers of Europe to sow division within the EU.

Offering war-torn Ukraine the prospect of EU membership and long-term financial support aims to deter Russian aggression further West, partly due to doubts about the United States' commitment to deterrence in Europe. The EU has granted candidate status to these countries to strengthen them in material terms while at the same time bolstering European credibility and deterrence. But it is not surprising that to deliver that agenda effectively, the EU also embarked on several projects to pool together more resources to upgrade its defense capacities as well as to invest in a strengthened CFSP according to a logic of strategic autonomy. European institutions and member states recognize the costs and challenges expansion will impose on their organization and its members. They also recognize that the alternative of providing security without a membership prospect lacks credibility and that a failure to provide security is not a viable alternative given the costs involved. Alongside institutional reform, enlargement is how the EU can avoid the tragedy of the commons.

Abbreviations

BTO	Brussels Treaty Organization
CAP	Common Agricultural Policy
CEN	European Committee for Standardization
CENELEC	European Committee for Electrotechnical Standardization
CFSP	Common Foreign and Security Policy
ECB	European Central Bank
ECSC	European Coal and Steel Community
EEA	European Economic Area
EEC	European Economic Community
EMS	European Monetary System
ERM	Exchange Rate Mechanism
ESDP	European Security and Defence Policy
EU	European Union
IMF	International Monetary Fund
NATO	North Atlantic Treaty Organization
NGOs	non-governmental organizations
SS-20	Soviet intermediate-range nuclear weapon
U.S.	United States
UK	United Kingdom
WEU	West European Union

References

Ahrens, Joachim, Herman W. Hoen, and Renate Ohr (2005). 'Deepening Integration in an Enlarged EU: A Club–Theoretical Perspective'. *Journal of European Integration* 27:4, pp. 417–439.

Alexander, Kern (2020). 'Financial Market Integration and EMU'. In Fabian Ambtenbrink and Christoph Herman, eds. *The EU Law of Economic and Monetary Union*. Oxford: Oxford University Press, pp. 1049–1069.

Anghel, Veronica (2020). 'Together or Apart?' *Survival* 62:3, pp. 179–202.

Anghel, Veronica (2025). *Global Risks to the EU*. Florence: European University Institute.

Anghel, Veronica, and Erik Jones (2022). 'Failing Forward in Eastern Enlargement: Problem Solving through Problem Making'. *Journal of European Public Policy* 29:7, pp. 1092–1111.

Anghel, Veronica, and Erik Jones (2024). 'The Transatlantic Relationship and the Russia-Ukraine War'. *Political Science Quarterly* 139:4, pp. 509–528.

Anghel, Veronica, and Erik Jones (2025). 'The Enlargement of International Organisations'. *West European Politics* 48:1, pp. 1–28.

Anghel, Veronica, and Jelena Džankić (2023). 'Wartime EU: Consequences of the Russia – Ukraine War on the Enlargement Process'. *Journal of European Integration* 45:3, pp. 487–501.

Axelrod, Robert (1984). *The Evolution of Cooperation*. New York: Basic Books.

Bauerle Danzman, Sarah, and Sophie Meunier (2023). 'Naïve No More: Foreign Direct Investment Screening in the European Union'. *Global Policy* 14:S3, pp. 40–53.

Benediktsdottir, Sigridur, Jon Danielsson, and Gylfi Zoega (2011). 'Lessons from the Collapse of a Financial System'. *Economic Policy* 26:66, pp. 183–235.

Blanchard, Olivier, and Francesco Giavazzi (2002). 'Current Account Deficits in the Euro Area: The End of the Feldstein-Horioka Puzzle?' *Brookings Papers on Economic Activity* 2, pp. 147–209.

Börzel, Tanja (2005). 'Mind the Gap! European Integration Between Level and Scope'. *Journal of European Public Policy* 12:2, pp. 217–236.

Brummer, Chris (2008). 'Regional Integration and Incomplete Club Goods: A Trade Perspective'. *Chicago Journal of International Law* 8:2, pp. 535–551.

Buchanan, James M. (1965). 'An Economic Theory of Clubs'. *Economica* 32:125, pp. 1–14.
Buck, Susan J. (2017). *The Global Commons: An Introduction*. London: Routledge.
Buti, Marco, and Sergio Fabbrini (2023). 'Next Generation EU and the Future of Economic Governance: Towards a Paradigm Change or Just a Big One-Off?' *Journal of European Public Policy* 30:4, pp. 676–695.
Buzan, Berry, Ole Wæver, Jaap de Wilde (1998). *Security: A New Framework for Analysis*. London: Lynne Rienner.
Cecchini, Paolo (1988). *The European Challenge, 1992: The Benefits of a Single Market*. Aldershot: Wildwood House.
Chang, Michele (2023). 'Economic Governance'. In Erik Jones and Masha Hedberg, eds. *Europe Today: A Twenty-First Century Introduction*. Lanham: Rowman & Littlefield, pp. 301–324.
Cornes, Richard, and Todd Sandler (1994). 'Are Public Goods Myths?' *Journal of Theoretical Politics* 6:3, pp. 369–385.
Cornes, Richard, and Todd Sandler (2012). *The Theory of Externalities, Public Goods, and Club Goods*, 2nd Edition. Cambridge: Cambridge University Press.
Cowles, Maria Green (2003). 'Non-State Actors and False Dichotomies: Reviewing IR/IPE Approaches to European Integration'. *Journal of European Public Policy* 10:1, pp. 102–120.
Coyle, Diane (2021). *Cogs and Monsters: What Economics Is, and What It Should Be*. Princeton: Princeton University Press.
Damro, Chad (2012). 'Market Power Europe'. *Journal of European Public Policy* 19:5, pp. 682–699.
Dandashly, Assem, and Amy Verdun (2021). 'Euro Adoption Policies in the Second Decade – The Remarkable Cases of the Baltic States'. In David Howarth and Amy Verdun, eds. *Economic and Monetary Union at Twenty: A Stocktaking of a Tumultuous Second Decade*. London: Routledge, pp. 93–109.
Davis Cross, Mai'a K., and Ireneusz Pawel Karolewski (2017). 'What Type of Power has the EU Exercised in the Ukraine–Russia Crisis? A Framework of Analysis'. *JCMS: Journal of Common Market Studies* 55:1, pp. 3–19.
Davis, Christina and Meredith Wilf (2017). 'Joining the Club: Accession to the GATT/ WTO'. *Journal of Politics* 79:3, pp. 964–978.
De Bièvre, Dirk (2006). 'The EU Regulatory Trade Agenda and the Quest for WTO Enforcement'. *Journal of European Public Policy* 13:6, pp. 847–862.

De Grauwe, Paul (2010). 'The Banking Crisis: Causes and Remedies'. In Leila Simona Talani, ed. *The Global Crash: Towards a New Global Financial Regime?* Basingstoke: Palgrave, pp. 10–31.

De Larosière, Jacques (2009). 'The High-Level Group of Financial Supervision in the EU'. Brussels: European Commission.

De Witte, Bruno (2002). 'Anticipating the Institutional Consequences of Expanded Membership of the European Union'. *International Political Science Review* 23:3, pp. 235–248.

Della Sala, Vincent (1998). 'Hollowing Out and Hardening the State: European Integration and the Italian Economy'. *West European Politics* 20:1, pp. 14–33.

Delors, Jacques (1989). 'Report on Economic and Monetary Union in the European Community'. Brussels: European Commission.

Demarais, Agathe (2022). *Backfire: How Sanctions Reshape the World Against U.S. Interests*. New York: Columbia University Press.

Deutsch, Karl W., Sidney A. Burrell, Robert A. Kann, et al. (1957). *Political Community and the North Atlantic Area: International Organization in Light of Historical Experience*. Princeton: Princeton University Press.

Draghi, Mario (2024). *The Future of European Competitiveness: Part A – A Competitiveness Strategy for Europe*. Brussels: European Commission (September).

Dyson, Tom (2016). 'Energy Security and Germany's Response to Russian Revisionism: The Dangers of Civilian Power'. *German Politics* 25:4, pp. 500–518.

Džankić, Jelena (2018). 'Immigrant Investor Programmes in the European Union (EU)'. *Journal of Contemporary European Studies* 26:1, pp. 64–80.

Džankić, Jelena, Soeren Keil, and Marko Kmezić, eds. (2018). *The Europeanisation of the Western Balkans: A Failure of EU Conditionality?* London: Palgrave Macmillan.

Epstein, Rachel A. (2017). *Banking on Markets: The Transformation of Bank-State Ties in Europe & Beyond*. Oxford: Oxford University Press.

European Commission (1994). *Growth, Competitiveness, Employment: The Challenges and Ways Forward in the 21st Century – White Paper*. Brussels: European Commission.

European Commission (2014). *Communication from the Commission to the European Parliament and the Council: A New EU Framework to Strengthen the Rule of Law*. Brussels: European Commission, COM(2014) 158 final.

European Commission (2022). 'Convergence Report'. *Institutional Paper 179*. Brussels: European Commission.

European Council (2022). 'European Council Conclusions on Ukraine, the Membership Applications of Ukraine, the Republic of Moldova and Georgia, Western Balkans and External Relations'. Brussels: European Council, 23 June.

European Council (2023). 'European Council Meeting (14 and 15 December 2023): Conclusions'. Brussels: European Council, EUCO 20/23 (15 December).

Fagan, Gabriel, and Vitor Gaspar (2008). 'Macroeconomic Adjustment to Monetary Union'. *ECB Working Paper No. 946*. Frankfurt: European Central Bank (October).

Favell, Adrian, and Randall Hansen (2002). 'Markets against Politics: Migration, EU Enlargement, and the Idea of Europe'. *Journal of Ethnic and Migration Studies* 28:4, pp. 581–601.

Feldstein, Martin, and Charles Horioka (1980). 'Domestic Saving and International Capital Flows'. *The Economic Journal* 90:358, pp. 314–329.

Foldvary, Fred (1994). *Public Goods and Private Communities*. Aldershot: Edward Elgar.

Gavin, Francis J. (2015). 'Strategies of Inhibition: U.S. Grand Strategy, the Nuclear Revolution, and Nonproliferation'. *International Security* 40:1, pp. 9–46.

Gavin, Francis J. (2023). *The Taming of Scarcity and the Problems of Plenty Rethinking International Relations and American Grand Strategy in a New Era*. London: IISS Adelphi Series.

Giavazzi, Francesco, and Marco Pagano (1988). 'The Advantages of Tying One's Hands: EMS Discipline and Central Bank Credibility'. *European Economic Review* 32:5, pp. 1055–1075.

Giersch, Herbert (1985). 'Eurosclerosis'. *Kieler Diskussionsbeiträge, No. 112*. Kiel: Institute für Weltwirtschaft (October).

Gros, Daniel, and Niels Thygesen (1998). *European Monetary Integration: From the European Monetary System to Economic and Monetary Union, Second Edition*. London: Longman.

Gruber, Lloyd (2000). *Ruling the World: Power Politics and the Rise of Supranational Institutions*. Princeton: Princeton University Press.

Haas, Ernst (1968). *The Uniting of Europe: Political, Social, and Economic Forces, 1950–1957*. Notre Dame: University of Notre Dame Press.

Haas, Peter M., Robert O. Keohane, and Mark A. Levy, eds. (1993). *Institutions for the Earth: Sources of Effective International Environmental Protection*. Cambridge, MA: MIT Press.

Hansen, Peo (2021). *A Modern Migration Theory: An Alternative Economic Approach to Failed EU Policy*. London: Agenda Publishing.

Hardin, Garrett (1968). 'The Tragedy of the Commons: The Population Problem Has No Technical Solution; It Requires a Fundamental Extension in Morality'. *Science* 162, pp. 1243–1248.

Heipertz, Martin, and Amy Verdun (2010). *Ruling Europe: The Politics of the Stability and Growth Pact*. Cambridge: Cambridge University Press.

Heritier, Adrienne, ed. (2002). *Common Goods: Reinventing European and International Governance*. Lanham: Rowman & Littlefield.

Higgott, Richard A., Geoffrey R. D. Underhill, and Andreas Bieler, eds. (2000). *Non-State Actors and Authority in the Global System*. London: Routledge.

Hix, Simon, and Abdul Noury (2009). 'After Enlargement: Voting Patterns in the Sixth European Parliament'. *Legislative Studies Quarterly* 34:2, pp. 159–174.

Hoffmann, Andreas (2013). 'Carry Trades and Speculative Manias: Evidence from Central and Eastern Europe'. *Journal of Post Keynesian Economics* 36:1, pp. 15–29.

Hofmann, Stephanie C. (2013). *European Security in NATO's Shadow: Party Ideologies and Institution Building*. Cambridge: Cambridge University Press.

Hofmann, Stephanie C., Anamarija Andreska, Erna Burai, and Juanita Uribe (2023). 'Porous Organizational Boundaries and Associated States: Introducing Memberness in International Organizations'. *European Journal of International Relations* 29:4, pp. 929–959.

Högenauer, Anna-Lena, David Howarth, and Lucia Quaglia (2023). 'Introduction to the Special Issue: The Persistent Challenges to European Banking Union'. *Journal of European Integration* 45:1, pp. 1–14.

Hooghe, Liesbet, and Gary Marks (2010). 'Types of Multi-level Governance'. In Henrik Enderlein, Sonja Wälti, Michael Zürn, eds. *Handbook on Multi-level Governance*. Cheltenham: Edward Elgar, pp. 17–31.

Hooghe, Liesbet, and Gary Marks (2019). 'Grand Theories of European Integration in the Twenty-First Century'. *Journal of European Public Policy* 26:8, pp. 1113–1133.

Howarth, David, and Lucia Quaglia (2016). *The Political Economy of European Banking Union*. Oxford: Oxford University Press.

Howorth, Jolyon (2012). 'European Security Institutions 1945–2010'. In Sven Biscop and Richard G. Whitman, eds. *The Routledge Handbook of European Security*. New York: Routledge, pp. 5–17.

Jones, Erik (2009). 'The Euro and the Financial Crisis'. *Survival* 51:2, pp. 41–54.

Jones, Erik (2015). 'The Forgotten Financial Union: How You Can Have a Euro Crisis without a Euro'. In Matthias Matthijs and Mark Blyth, eds. *The Future of the Euro*. New York: Oxford University Press, pp. 44–69.

Jones, Erik (2016). 'Confronting Europe's Single Market'. *Survival* 58:1, pp. 59–67.

Jones, Erik (2018). 'Toward a Theory of Disintegration'. *Journal of European Public Policy* 25:3, pp. 440–451.

Juncker, Jean-Claude, Donald Tusk, Jeroen Dijsselbloom, Mario Draghi, and Martin Schulz (2015). *Completing Europe's Economic and Monetary Union*. Brussels: European Commission.

Kaiser, Wolfram, and Jürgen Elvert, eds. (2004). *European Union Enlargement: A Comparative History*. London: Routledge.

Kelemen, R. Daniel (2019). 'Is Differentiation Possible in Rule of Law?' *Comparative European Studies* 17:2, pp. 246–260.

Kelemen, R. Daniel, Anand Menon, and Jonathan Slapin (2014a). 'Wider and Deeper? Enlargement and Integration in the European Union'. *Journal of European Public Policy* 21:5, pp. 647–663.

Kelemen, R. Daniel, Anand Menon, and Jonathan Slapin (2014b). 'The European Union: Wider and Deeper?' *Journal of European Public Policy* 21:5, pp. 643–646.

Keohane, Robert (2010). 'Review Symposium: Beyond the Tragedy of the Commons'. *Perspectives on Politics* 8:2, pp. 577–580.

Keohane, Robert O., and Elinor Ostrom, eds. (1994). *Local Commons and Global Interdependence*. New York: Sage.

Kindleberger, Charles P. (1986). *The World in Depression, Revised and Enlarged Edition*. Berkeley: University of California Press.

Kok, Wim (2004). *Facing the Challenge: The Lisbon Strategy for Growth and Employment*. Brussels: European Commission, November.

König, Thomas, and Thomas Bräuninger (2004). 'Accession and Reform of the European Union: A Game-Theoretical Analysis of Eastern Enlargement and the Constitutional Reform'. *European Union Politics* 5:4, pp. 419–439.

Kopstein, Jeffrey, and David Reilly (2006). 'As Europe Gets Larger, Will It Disappear?' *International Studies Review* 8:1, pp. 140–150.

Krahmann, Elke (2008). 'Security: Collective Good or Commodity?' *European Journal of International Relations* 14:3, pp. 379–404.

Krasner, Stephen D. (1983). *International Regimes*. Ithaca: Cornell University Press.

Kuus, Merje (2007). *Geopolitics Reframed: Security and Identity in Europe's Eastern Enlargement*. London: Palgrave Macmillan.

Lamfalussy, Alexandre (2001). *Final Report of the Committee of Wise Men on the Regulation of European Securities Markets*. Brussels: European Commission.

Larsen, Signe Rehling (2021). *The Constitutional Theory of the Federation of the European Union*. Oxford: Oxford University Press.

Letta, Enrico (2024). *Much More than a Market: Speed, Security, Solidarity*. Brussels: Council of the European Union (April).

Leuffen, Dirk, Berthold Rittberger, and Frank Schimmelfennig (2022). *Integration and Differentiation in the European Union: Theory and Policies*, Second Edition. London: Palgrave McMillan.

Ludlow, Peter (1982). *The Making of the European Monetary System: A Case Study in the Politics of the European Community*. London: Butterworths Scientific.

Marjolin, Robert (1975). *Report of the Study Group 'Economic and Monetary Union 1980'*. Brussels: Commission of the European Communities.

Marks, Gary (2011). 'Europe and Its Empires: From Rome to the European Union'. *Journal of Common Market Studies* 50:1, pp. 1–20.

Mattli, Walter (1999). *The Logic of Regional Integration*. Cambridge: Cambridge University Press.

McCarthy, Patrick (1990). 'France Faces Reality: *Rigueur* and the Germans'. In David P. Calleo and Claudia Morgenstern, eds. *Recasting Europe's Economies: National Strategies in the 1980s*. Lanham: University Press of America, pp. 25–78.

McCormick, John (2007). *The European Superpower*. London: Palgrave Macmillan.

McNamara, Kathleen R. (1993). 'Common Markets, Uncommon Currencies: System Effects and the European Community'. In Jack Snyder and Robert Jervis, eds. *Coping with Complexity in the International System*. Boulder: Westview, pp. 303–327.

Meadows, Donella (2015). *Thinking In Systems*. New York: Chelsea Green.

Mérand, Frédéric (2008). *European Defense Policy Beyond the Member State*. Oxford: Oxford University Press.

Merler, Silvia, and Jean Pisani-Ferry (2012). 'Sudden Stops in the Euro Area'. *Bruegel Policy Contribution, Issue 2012/06*. Brussels: Bruegel (March).

Miles, Lee (1995). 'Enlargement of the European Union and the Nordic Model'. *Journal of European Integration* 19:1, pp. 43–69.

Mitchell, John D. B. (1976). 'The Tindemans Report, Retrospect and Prospect'. *Common Market Law Review* 13:4, pp. 455–484.

Moravcsik, Andrew, and Milada Vachudova (2003). 'National Interests, State Power, and EU Enlargement'. *East European Politics and Societies* 17:1, pp. 42–57.

Moses, Jonathon (2017). *Eurobondage: The Political Costs of Monetary Union in Europe*. Colchester: ECPR Press.

Mügge, Daniel (2010). *Widen the Market, Narrow the Competition: Banker Interests and the Making of a European Capital Market*. Colchester: ECPR Press.

Murdoch, James C., and Todd Sandler (1984). 'Complementarity, Free Riding, and the Military Expenditures of NATO Allies'. *Journal of Public Economics* 25, pp. 83–101.

Myrdal, Gunnar (1956). *An International Economy: Problems and Prospects*. New York: Harper & Brothers.

Niinistö, Sauli (2024). *Safer Together: Strengthening Europe's Civilian and Military Preparedness and Readiness*. Brussels: European Commission (October).

Novaković, Igor, and Tanja Plavšić (2024). *An Analysis of Serbia's Alignment with the European Union's Foreign Policy Declarations and Measures: Annual Review for 2023*. Belgrade: International and Security Affairs Center.

Olson, Mancur (1965). *The Logic of Collective Action: Public Goods and the Theory of Groups*. Cambridge, MA: Harvard University Press.

Olson, Mancur and Richard Zeckhauser (1966). 'An Economic Theory of Alliances'. *Review of Economics and Statistics* 48, pp. 266–279.

Orenstein, Mitchell A., and R. Daniel Kelemen (2017). 'Trojan Horses in EU Foreign Policy'. *JCMS: Journal of Common Market Studies* 55:1, pp. 87–102.

Ostrom, Elinor (1990). *Governing the Commons: The Evolution of Institutions for Collective Action*. Cambridge: Cambridge University Press.

Ostrom, Elinor (2003). 'How Types of Goods and Property Rights Jointly Affect Collective Action'. *Journal of Theoretical Politics* 15:3, pp. 239–270.

Ostrom, Elinor (2005). *Understanding Institutional Diversity*. Princeton: Princeton University Press.

Ostrom, Elinor (2008). 'The Challenge of Common-Pool Resources'. *Environment: Science and Policy for Sustainable Development* 50:4, pp. 8–21.

Ostrom, Elinor, Joanna Burger, Christopher B. Field, Richard B. Norgaard, and David Policansky (1999). 'Revisiting the Commons: Local Lessons, Global Challenges'. *Science* 284:5412, pp. 278–282.

Padoa-Schioppa, Tommaso (1987). *Efficiency, Stability and Equity: A Strategy for the Evolution of the Economic System of the European Community*. Brussels: Commission of the European Communities, II/49/87 (April).

Pelkmans, Jacques (1987). 'The New Approach to Technical Harmonization and Standardization'. *Journal of Common Market Studies* 25:3, pp. 249–269.

Pelle, Anita, András London, and Éva Kuruczleki (2021). 'The European Union: A Dynamic Complex System of Clubs Comprised by Countries Performing a Variety of Capitalism'. *Forum for Social Economics* 50:4, pp. 530–552.

Pierret, Laura, and David Howarth (2023). 'Moral Hazard, Central Bankers, and Banking Union: Profession Dissensus and the Politics of European Financial Stability'. *Journal of European Integration* 45:1, pp. 15–41.

Piroska, Dóra, and Rachel A. Epstein (2023). 'Stalled by Design: New Paradoxes in the European Union's Single Financial Market'. *Journal of European Integration* 45:1, pp. 181–201.

Popova, Maria, and Oxana Shevel (2023). *Russia and Ukraine: Entangled Histories, Diverging States.* Cambridge, MA: Polity.

Posner, Elliot (2007). 'Financial Transformation in the European Union'. In Sophie Meunier and Kathleen R. McNamara, eds. *Making History: European Integration and Institutional Change at Fifty.* Oxford: Oxford University Press, pp. 139–158.

Prebisch, Raúl (1962). 'The Economic Development of Latin America and Its Principal Problems'. *Economic Bulletin for Latin America* 7:1, pp. 1–22.

Preston, Christopher (1997). *Enlargement and Integration in the European Union.* London: Routledge.

Radaelli, Claudio (2003). *The Open Method of Coordination: A New Governance Architecture for the European Union?* Stockholm: Swedish Institute for European Policy Studies.

Rothschild, Emma (1995). 'What is Security?' *Daedalus* 124:3, pp. 53–98.

Ruggie, John Gerard (1982). 'International Regimes, Transactions, and Change: Embedded Liberalism in the Postwar Economic Order'. *International Organization* 36:2, pp. 379–415.

Sandler, Todd (1977). 'Impurity of Defense: An Application to the Economics of Alliances'. *Kyklos* 30, pp. 443–460.

Sandler, Todd (1982). 'A Theory of Intergenerational Clubs'. *Economic Inquiry* 20:2, pp. 191–208.

Sandler, Todd (1993). 'The Economic Theory of Alliances'. *Journal of Conflict Resolution* 37, pp. 446–483.

Sandler, Todd (2006). 'Regional Public Goods and International Organizations'. *Review of International Organizations* 1, pp. 5–25.

Sandler, Todd (2013). 'Buchanan Clubs'. *Constitutional Political Economy* 24, pp. 265–284.

Sandler, Todd, and John F. Forbes (1980). 'Burden Sharing, Strategy, and the Design of NATO'. *Economic Inquiry* 18, pp. 425–444.

Sandler, Todd, and John T. Tschirhart (1980). 'The Economic Theory of Clubs: An Evaluative Survey'. *Journal of Economic Literature* 18:4, pp. 1481–1521.

Sandler, Todd, and John T. Tschirhart (1997). 'Club theory: Thirty Years Later'. *Public Choice* 93:3, pp. 335–355.

Schimmelfennig, Frank (2001). 'Liberal Identity and Postnationalist Inclusion: The Eastern Enlargement of the European Union'. In Lars-Erik Cederman, ed. *Constructing Europe's Identity: The External Dimension*. Boulder: Lynne Rienner Publishers, pp. 165–186.

Schimmelfennig, Frank, Dirk Leuffen, and Berthold Rittberger (2015). 'The European Union as a System of Differentiated Integration: Interdependence, Politicization and Differentiation'. *Journal of European Public Policy* 22:6, pp. 764–782.

Schimmelfennig, Frank, and Ulrich Sedelmeier (2002). 'Theorizing EU Enlargement: Research Focus, Hypotheses, and the State of Research'. *Journal of European Public Policy* 9:4, pp. 500–528.

Schmidt, Vivien A. (2024). 'Theorizing European Integration: The Four Phases Since Ernst Haas' Original Contribution'. *Journal of European Public Policy* 31:10, pp. 3346–3371.

Schmitter, Philippe C. (1969). 'Three Neo-Functional Hypotheses about International Integration'. *International Organization* 23:1, pp. 161–166.

Schmitter, Philippe C. (1996). 'Imagining the Future of the Euro-Polity With the Help of New Concepts'. In G. Marks, F. Scharpf, P. Schmitter and W. Streeck, eds. *Governance in the European Union*. London: Sage, pp. 121–150.

Schneider, Christina J. (2008). *Conflict, Negotiation, and European Union Enlargement*. Cambridge: Cambridge University Press.

Schramm, Lucas (2024). 'Using Go-It-Alone Power to Overcome Intergovernmental Deadlock: National Vetoes, Credible Threats, and Multi-Speed Europe in the British Budgetary Rebate Crisis'. *Acta Politica* 59, pp. 847–865.

Segers, Mathieu (2023). *The Origins of European Integration: The Pre-History of Today's European Union, 1937–1951*. Cambridge: Cambridge University Press.

Servan-Schreiber, Jean-Jacques (1967). *Le défi américain*. Paris: Denoël.

Siddi, Marco (2016). 'German Foreign Policy towards Russia in the Aftermath of the Ukraine Crisis: A New *Ostpolitik*?' *Europe-Asia Studies* 68:4, pp. 665–677.

Silj, Alessandro (1967). 'Europe's Political Puzzle: A Study of the Fouchet Negotiations and the 1963 Veto'. *Occasional Papers in International Affairs no. 17*. Cambridge: Harvard Center for International Affairs.

Sloan, Stanley R. (2003). *NATO, the European Union, and the Atlantic Community: The Transatlantic Bargain Reconsidered*. Lanham: Rowman & Littlefield.

Snegovaya, Maria (2023). 'Why Russia's Democracy Never Began'. *Journal of Democracy* 34:3, pp. 105–18.

Södersten, Anna (2023). 'Rule of Law Crisis: EU in Limbo Between Federalism and Flexible Integration'. In Antonina Bakardjieva Engelbrekt, Per Ekman, Anna Michalska, and Lars Oxelheim, eds. *The EU Between Federal Union and Flexible Integration*. London: Palgrave Macmillan, pp. 51–74.

Stone-Sweet, Alec, and Wayne Sandholtz (1997). 'European Integration and Supranational Governance'. *Journal of European Public Policy* 4:3, pp. 297–317.

Stone-Sweet, Alec, and Wayne Sandholtz (1998). 'Integration, Supranational Governance, and the Institutionalization of the European Polity'. In Wayne Sandholtz and Alec Stone-Sweet, eds. *European Integration and Supranational Governance*. Oxford: Oxford University Press, pp. 1–26.

Stone-Sweet, Alec, and Wayne Sandholtz (1999). 'European Integration and Supranational Governance Revisited: Rejoinder to Branch and Ohrgaard'. *Journal of European Public Policy* 6:1, pp. 144–154.

Story, Jonathan, and Ingo Walter (1997). *Political Economy of Financial Integration in Europe: The Battle of the Systems*. Cambridge, MA: MIT Press.

Teasdale, Anthony L. (1993). 'The Life and Death of the Luxembourg Compromise'. *Journal of Common Market Studies* 31:4, pp. 567–579.

Teasdale, Anthony L. (2016). 'The Fouchet Plan: De Gaulle's Intergovernmental Design for Europe'. *LSE 'Europe in Question' Discussion Paper Series* 117 (October), pp. 1–55.

Thomas, Daniel C. (2001). *The Helsinki Effect: International Norms, Human Rights, and the Demise of Communism*. Princeton: Princeton University Press.

Thorhallsson, Baldur, and Peadar Kirby (2012). 'Financial Crisis is Iceland and Ireland: Does European Union and Euro Membership Matter?' *Journal of Common Market Studies* 50:5, pp. 801–818.

Toshkov, Dimiter D. (2017). 'The Impact of the Eastern Enlargement on the Decision-Making Capacity of the European Union'. *Journal of European Public Policy* 24:2, pp. 177–196.

Tsoukalis, Loukas (1977). *The Politics and Economics of European Monetary Integration*. London: Routledge.

Underhill, Geoffrey R., and Erik Jones (2023). 'Optimum Financial Areas: Retooling the Governance of Global Finance'. *The World Economy* 46:6, pp. 1582–1608.

Vachudova, Milada A. (2005). *Europe Undivided: Democracy, Leverage, and Integration After Communism*. Oxford: Oxford University Press.

van der Veen, A. Maurits (2014). 'Enlargement and the Anticipatory Deepening of European Integration'. *Journal of European Public Policy* 21:5, pp. 761–775.

Van Rompuy, Herman (2014). *Europa in de Storm*. Leuven: Davidsfonds.

van Zeben, Josephine (2019). 'Polycentric Features of the European Union'. In Josephine van Zeben and Ana Bobić, eds. *Polycentricity in the European Union*. Cambridge: Cambridge University Press, pp. 28–50.

Vaughan, Diane (1999). 'The Dark Side of Organizations: Mistake, Misconduct, and Disaster'. *Annual Review of Sociology* 25, pp. 271–305.

Viñals, José, and Juan F. Jimeno (1998). 'Monetary Union and European Unemployment'. In Jeffry Frieden, Daniel Gros, and Erik Jones, eds. *The New Political Economy of EMU*. Lanham: Rowman & Littlefield, pp. 13–52.

Viola, Lora Anne (2020). *The Closure of the International System: How Institutions Create Political Equalities and Hierarchies*. Cambridge: Cambridge University Press.

Vogler, John (2012). 'Global Commons Revisited'. *Global Policy* 3.1, pp. 61–71.

Wallaschek, Stefan (2019). 'The Discursive Construction of Solidarity: Analyzing Public Claims in Europe's Migration Crisis'. *Political Studies* 68:1, pp. 74–92.

Wilkinson, Benedict (2020). 'The EU's Defense Technological and Industrial Base'. Brussels: European Parliament, PE 603.483.

Willis, F. Roy (1968). *France, Germany and the New Europe, 1945–1967*. Stanford: Stanford University Press.

Young, Alasdair R., and John Peterson (2014). *Parochial Global Europe: 21st Century Trade Politics*. Oxford: Oxford University Press.

Youngs, Richard (2024). *Geoliberal Europe and the Test of War*. London: Agenda Publishing.

Acknowledgments

We appreciate the many colleagues who generously dedicated their time to providing insightful feedback on various iterations of this manuscript. Their engagement in seminars and panel discussions at the Robert Schuman Center for Advanced Studies of the European University Institute, as well as at various professional organizations, has been invaluable. We are especially grateful to the three reviewers, whose thoughtful critiques significantly strengthened our argument, and to the series editor, Nauro F. Campos, for his guidance and support. This project has received funding from the European Union's Horizon Europe research and innovation program under grant agreement No. 101079219.

Cambridge Elements =

Economics of European Integration

Nauro F. Campos
University College London and ETH-Zürich

Nauro F. Campos is Professor of Economics at University College London and Research Professor at ETH-Zürich. His main fields of interest are political economy and European integration. He has previously taught at CERGE-EI (Prague), California (Fullerton), Newcastle, Brunel, Bonn, Paris 1 Sorbonne and Warwick. He was a visiting Fulbright Fellow at Johns Hopkins (Baltimore), a Robert McNamara Fellow at The World Bank, and a CBS Fellow at Oxford. He is currently a Research Fellow at IZA-Bonn, a Professorial Fellow at UNU-MERIT (Maastricht University), a member of the Scientific Advisory Board of the (Central) Bank of Finland, and a Senior Fellow of the ESRC Peer Review College. He was a visiting scholar at the University of Michigan, ETH, USC, Bonn, UCL, Stockholm, IMF, World Bank, and the European Commission. From 2009 to 2014, he was seconded as Senior Economic Advisor/SRF to the Chief Economist of the UK's Department for International Development. He received his Ph.D. from the University of Southern California (Los Angeles) in 1997, where he was lucky enough to learn about institutions from Jeff Nugent and Jim Robinson and (more than) happy to be Dick Easterlin's RA. He is the editor in chief of Comparative Economic Studies, the journal of the Association for Comparative Economic Studies.

About the Series

This Element series provides authoritative, up-to-date reviews of core topics and recent developments in the field with particular emphasis on structural, policy and political economy issues. State-of-the-art contributions explore topics such as labour mobility, the euro crisis, Brexit, immigration, inequality, international trade, unemployment, climate change policy, and more.

Cambridge Elements

Economics of European Integration

Elements in the Series

The Road to Monetary Union
Richard Pomfret

Completing a Genuine Economic and Monetary Union
Iain Begg

Europe and the Transformation of the Irish Economy
John FitzGerald and Patrick Honohan

The Happiness Revolution in Europe
Richard Ainley Easterlin and Kelsey James O'Connor

From Club to Commons: Enlargement, Reform and Sustainability in European Integration
Veronica Anghel and Erik Jones

A full series listing is available at www.cambridge.org/EEI

For EU product safety concerns, contact us at Calle de José Abascal, 56–1°,
28003 Madrid, Spain or eugpsr@cambridge.org.

www.ingramcontent.com/pod-product-compliance
Lightning Source LLC
LaVergne TN
LVHW011851060526
838200LV00054B/4282